The Iron Road of Franconia

To JANET & PAUL,

The Iron Road

A History of the RF&P Railroad in Fairfax County

By Nathaniel Lee

Printed by CreateSpace

North Charleston, South Carolina

2016

First printing: April 2016
International Standard Book Number:

   (ISBN-10) 153 – 0919584

   (EAN-13) 978 – 1530919581

CreateSpace Independent Publishing Platform
North Charleston, South Carolina, USA

Copies of this book are available for purchase online at:
http://www.createspace.com/6190241

The author gladly accepts any error corrections found within this book. The author recognizes that some words and company names are the property of the trademark holder. The author uses them for identification purposes only. This is not an official publication of any railroad company.

The typeface used in this publication is Garamond, which offers elegance and readability. Claude Garamond (1480–1561) was a French publisher and type designer whose designs are the basis for many modern Garamond versions. Robert Slimbach created this version released by Adobe Incorporated in 1989. Its italics are the designs of Claude Garamond's assistant, Robert Granjon.

To Milton Wayne Lee,
who is always my sturdy iron road.

CONTENTS

LEADERS OF THE LINE

- **Alexandria and Fredericksburg Railway Co. (1870 – 1890)**
  - Pennsylvania Railroad Management
    - John Edgar Thomson (1870 – 1874)
    - Thomas Alexander Scott (1874 – 1880)
    - George Brooke Roberts (1880 – 1890)
- **Washington Southern Railway Company (1890 – 1920)**
  - Pennsylvania Railroad Management
    - George Brooke Roberts (1890 – 1896)
    - Frank Thomson (1897 – 1899)
    - Alexander J. Cassatt (1899 – 1901)
  - Richmond, Fredericksburg and Potomac Railroad
    - E. D. T. Myers (1901 – 1905)
    - William J. Leake (1905 – 1907)
    - William White (1907 – 1920)
- **Richmond – Washington Company (1920 – 1991)**
  - Richmond, Fredericksburg and Potomac Railroad
    - Eppa Hunton, Jr. (1920 – 1932)
    - Norman Call (1932 – 1955)
    - William T. Rice (1955 – 1957)
    - Wirt P. Marks, Jr. (1957 – 1960)
    - Stuart Schumate (1961 – 1981)
    - John J. Newbauer, Jr. (1981 – 1985)
    - Richard L. Beadles (1985 – 1986)
    - Frank A. Crovo, Jr. (1986 – 1991)
- **C. S. X. Corporation (1991 – 2016)**
  - C. S. X. Transportation Management
    - John W. Snow (1991 – 2003)
    - Michael J. Ward (2003 – 2016)

RAILROAD STATION MAP

The map below traces the course that the Alexandria and Fredericksburg Railway followed through Fairfax County, Virginia. The stations, spur lines and major points of interest discussed in the book can be found on the map below.

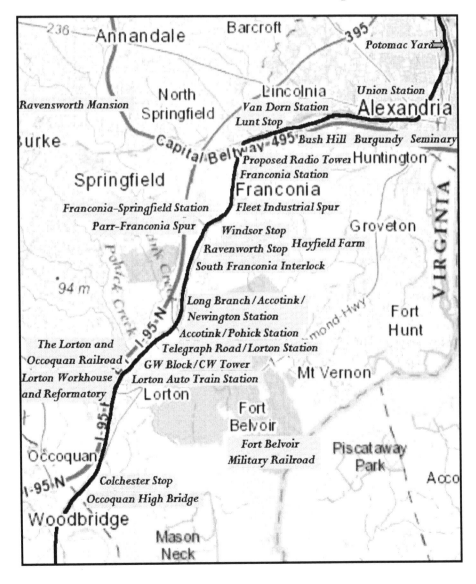

Chapter One

THE SOUTHERN GATEWAY

ℰℭ

*"One stretch of track was so crooked
we met ourselves coming back."*
– Noah Braunstein

ℰℭ

Attempts by the Pennsylvania Railroad to enter into the rail system of the South in 1870 were controversial, both politically and financially. The Southern people were still sore from their loss in the American Civil War less than a decade before. They were not going to greet Northerners with open arms, especially when they proposed to wipe out the local markets that many of the Southern railroad companies and small towns had built. In expanding their territory into the South, Pennsylvania Railroad leaders were wise enough to work directly with Southerners, or at least with investors whose business had them frequently crossing over the Mason–Dixon Line. In spite of that, Southerners still blamed them of partaking in the worst political, economic and ethical dishonesty in order to rob the South of its economic independence. Such claims were mostly undeserved, but they still hung around for decades.[1]

The topography and the economy of the South guaranteed that its railroads would have noticeable differences from the railroads in the North. In colonial days, Virginia's economic power was in the farming of cash crops, predominantly tobacco. Cotton would not become an important crop until the early nineteenth century. However, this focus on cash crops quickly made the South very one-dimensional and dependent on the success of these crops. Enslaved African Americans carried out a good deal of the farming, but sizable numbers of poor whites also worked in the fields, often at the side of slaves and free blacks. Workers then normally loaded their crops on small boats for a trip down the river to meet coastal or oceangoing ships.

The plantation economy system had produced a string of small, shallow ports all along the Southern seaboard with the sole purpose of shipping tobacco to Europe. Few of these towns had any great economic worth, and yet the people residing in every town with a harbor dreamed that they could start one of the South's great trading centers, if only they had access to better transportation to the farms in the west, away from easy river access. The State of Virginia funded a ton of public projects with this in mind, spending more than any other state. In 1816, the Virginia General Assembly created the Board of Public Works. This bureau spent over fourteen million dollars in state tax revenues throughout the rest of the antebellum era to build turnpikes, canals and railroads.[2]

The Industrial Revolution changed the types of goods available to local markets. By increasing transportation speed with steamboats and railroads, farmers could sell crops to far-off cities without their produce spoiling during the trip, stimulating economic growth in their local communities. Prior to the introduction of steam power into society, farmers only produced enough crops to feed their family and pay their debts. Now, farmers focused instead on crops that would bring the highest price at market, confident that their crops could get there quickly. Crops flowed north, and factory goods flowed south.

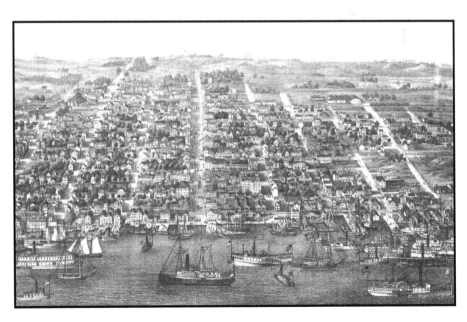

"A Bird's Eye View of Alexandria, Virginia" by mapmaker
Charles Magnus depicts the thriving port city in 1863.[3]

The State of Virginia never had any grand vision or strategic plan in developing its early railroads. In fact, the first railroads ran for just a few miles between farms and rivers, with people still favoring the colonial-era transport model. However, in Fairfax County, the normal condition of the roadways was reason enough to praise the new railroads. Winter rains and spring thaws routinely made farm roads virtually impassible. The two railroads traversing Fairfax County in 1870 included the Washington and Ohio Railroad that served the towns of Falls Church and Herndon, and the Orange, Alexandria and Manassas Railroad that served Springfield and Clifton.[4]

The railroads tied Virginia into a broader national marketplace, with everything from food to furniture now appearing in local shops and homes. Yet, Southerners generally considered their railroads to be a piece of the local economy serving their local needs, rather than a part of some larger regional or national system. Most Southern railroads cut across lightly settled farmlands, with hardly enough traffic to keep a railroad company in business. The railroad companies themselves encouraged farmers to diversify the crops that they planted, so that the railroads could transport to more customers.

In order to deal with operating expenses, railroad administrators had few choices other than to charge higher fares. These high fares were only possible with a localized monopoly of the transportation system. The owners of each local railroad were extremely angry at any attempts by outsiders, even if they were fellow Southerners, to build a rival railroad line in their area. Also disliked were the railroads that only carried long distance trains, because they could charge prices below those the local railroads could live on. Owners even built railroads with different track widths, or "gauges" in a conscious effort to stop a rival railroad from being able to send rail cars on their tracks or build a through route around their territory. A great deal of the South's railroad system did use a standard five-foot gauge, but by the year 1871, there were over twenty different track gauges on the ground. It would take until 1886 and a massive public works project for the railroads to rebuild at the same gauge as their Northern counterparts.[5]

Setting the gauge issue aside, many small towns simply passed laws banning different railroads from joining their tracks together in their town. In so doing, local businesses made certain that their own town would forever stay a transfer point for travelers and cargo. Passengers would stop to spend money at shops, restaurants or hotels while all of their belongings were unloaded, hauled across town, and reloaded onto another train. By the year 1850, the railroad system in the South seemed well linked and far reaching on paper, but in reality, it consisted of many independent and isolated railroads, linked together by connections that actually failed to connect.

The few Southerners drawn into trying to sell railroads to wealthy investors ran into several substantial barriers. Most Southern wealth was in land and slaves, with little left over for other activities. The nation's biggest banks were also in the North, and their investments focused mostly on northern industrial markets. Europeans also were hesitant to invest in the badly developed transportation network of the South, and their distaste increased in proportion to the rise of abolitionist feelings in the United Kingdom and Europe at large. Finally, even though an accomplished and reliable group of railroad tradesmen had surfaced in the North as early as 1850, no such group was present in the South. The South's dependence on agriculture and slavery had left skilled labor in very short supply, with most of the engineers and mechanics coming in from the North.

The American Civil War raged for four years between 1861 and 1865 and left the railroad system of the South in a state of complete devastation, with twisted tracks, burned bridges and overworked engines. Virginians returned home to find rail cars and locomotives badly maintained, destroyed by war or confiscated by the invading Union forces. Little money was on hand to fix the damage, especially as the South had just lost both its investment in slaves and now faced a looming Confederate war debt. State governments, which had financed a substantial part of the railroad construction budgets in the past, were no longer in any situation to offer money for rebuilding or expansion projects.

It was shortly after the war in 1869, when lawmakers broached their concerns about the considerable debt that the state government had racked up in previous years from bad investments in canals and turnpikes. The fear of incurring yet more state debt prompted lawmakers to add Article X, Section 10 to the new state constitution. Known as the internal improvement clause, it prohibits state funding for all internal improvements, with the exception of roads and parks. Ironically, all the railroads owned by the state on the eve of the Civil War were actually generating good income for the state government.[6]

The government sold most of its railroad stocks at auction to Northern companies, since they had cash to spare. The state government kept stock in only one railroad line, the Richmond, Fredericksburg and Potomac Railroad Company. Moving forward into the Reconstruction era, this constitutional provision actually hampered railroad development and opened the door to Northern railroad companies to control how the state's transportation and economy would develop. In the case of airports, shipping ports and railroads, this left the state of Virginia in a curious position on how to upgrade its public infrastructure legally on private property. Though challenged as recently as 2011, the Supreme Court of Virginia has upheld the provision.

Edwin Forbes' sketch depicts the RF&P R.R. Bridge over the Rappahannock River at Fredericksburg under repair on May 6, 1862 by Union Army engineers.[7]

With no funding assistance coming from the government for the now privately held railroad companies, some railroad owners in the South realized that all the infighting between neighboring railroad companies was going to drag all of their companies into financial ruin. Therefore, they tried to create income by imitating what their counterparts in the North had done, building special long-distance lines for through traffic. More commerce would allow the owners from the biggest railroad company in each area to rebuild. They could buy more equipment and pay a profit to their investors. In building these long-distance routes, railroad executives did exactly what they swore they would never do prior to the war. They destroyed the many local monopolies that had distinguished the antebellum era. Railroad companies that were not able to play a part in building these new long-distance routes were almost certain to find a drop in traffic and profits.[8]

As the year 1870 approached, Virginians in particular had plenty of cause to be anxious, for reasons that went further than just their military defeat by Ulysses S. Grant and his Union armies. New inventions, such as the steamship and the telegraph, lowered commodity prices and meant that more farming profits went to Northern cities where the nation's vast majority of factories were located. Southern self-reliance declined as a dependency on Northern manufactured goods increased, and a family's personal finances became more dependent on market forces. To many, the promise of new industry seemed more a pretense used to interfere than an actual economic improvement plan.

Northern banks, as well as European investors, expressed anxiety at the financial and political disorder that characterized the Reconstruction South and were not as eager to give out loans to farmers. Those actions affected not just the farmers but other local businesses as well. Local business leaders often bitterly opposed the entry of other businesses into their territory, particularly if those strangers were in any way tied to economic interests in the North.

People who had once cheered on railroad construction when it pledged to mix more local power with more economic benefits saw no good explanation why their local transportation infrastructure should be under the control of the Northern capitalists, men who seemingly wanted nothing less than to bleed dry the economic lifeblood of the South. That way of thinking, added on top of the boiling war anger, racial conflict, and the political confusion over the formation of Reconstruction-era governments, guaranteed that when the Pennsylvania Railroad, one of the biggest and most iconic of Northern institutions, became involved in the South, they would be walking into a hornet's nest.

Nevertheless, into this breach came the visionary Pennsylvania Railroad President John Edgar Thomson. Later nicknamed the "Father of the Pennsylvania Railroad," Thomson would be the driving force behind his railroad expanding southward from Pennsylvania into Maryland and Virginia. He was born near Philadelphia, Pennsylvania in 1804. He grew up at the start of the great industrial revolution that would change America into a world power. Thomson had a love for solving complex problems that would lead him into engineering and the growing railroad business.

He began his career with the Philadelphia and Columbia Rail Yards survey crew, which plotted the path for railroad tracks through rough wilderness. Thomson soon proved to be a quick study and expert surveyor. By the age of 26, he was already the chief engineer of the new Georgia Railroad. Under his leadership, tracks stretched from Augusta to Atlanta, a record setting 173 miles, the longest railroad in the world at the time.[9]

Pennsylvania Railroad President John Edgar Thomson (1804 – 1874).[10]

Thomson soon after accepted a position as chief engineer with the Pennsylvania Railroad and in 1852 rose to the position of President. Under his 22-year leadership, the railroad prospered and built nearly 6,000 miles of new track, including the tracks that run through the Franconia community in Fairfax County today. The Pennsylvania Railroad became the largest railroad in the world and saw its profits rise from $617,000 in 1852 to $8.2 million in 1874.[11]

Thomson was highly regarded by the people he worked with for his honesty and dedication. Thomson never had children, but held a deep affection for his adopted niece Charlotte Foster, an orphan since childhood. This affection was evident after he passed away in 1874. He created a foundation in his will that still operates to this day. It provides for the housing, care and education of daughters of railroad employees who died in the line of duty.

Thomson recognized that the building of tracks was not the issue, but the politics in Virginia. In order to expand the Pennsylvania Railroad into the South, Thomson had to win the game of politics and keep his involvement in the shadows. To reveal that a large Northern railroad was taking over Southern railroads would galvanize the Southern people against him. There was already a well-known term in circulation for such a person, "carpetbagger." His solution was one that worked in Pennsylvania a decade earlier: a holding company. This way, Thomson need only own half of the stock in a railroad (or less) in order to have sufficient advantage to choose board members and influence policies.

In 1871, the Southern Railway Security Company quietly formed in New York City, and the Pennsylvania Railroad began purchasing railroad companies all over the map. Historian Trina Rossman described it best as "a complicated spree of leases, stock buyouts, loans and construction projects involving at least fourteen different companies. The result was an administrative and financial rat's nest of unparalleled size." The impact was profound. A railroad company could now avoid compiling with the laws in one state, simply by becoming a part of a company in another state. Thomson and his partner, Thomas Scott, were both visionaries far ahead of their time. No state in the Union had yet legalized or regulated the business concept of a holding company.[12]

Chapter Two

THE LONG WAY AROUND

ဢၮ

"If the track is tough and the hill is rough,
thinking you can just ain't enough!"
– Shel Silverman

ဢၮ

In 1872, the Pennsylvania Railroad stretched as far south as the District of Columbia. For J. Edgar Thomson and the idealistic leaders of the Pennsylvania Railroad, Washington was not the end of the tracks, but the doorway to the South. Just over the Potomac River in Virginia lay a railway system, not as far-reaching as that in the North, now shattered by four years of war. However, it held potential and the Pennsylvania Railroad greatly needed Southern economic traffic. After General Robert E. Lee surrendered his army at Appomattox

Courthouse, the city of Washington quickly settled back into its prewar slumber, with few regular passenger trains required and even less freight traffic. Washington was far from the large bustling city of today. In the middle of the nineteenth century, it was still a small town trying to grow into the grand designs of Pierre L'Enfant, its majestic marble monuments still under construction. Pennsylvania Railroad President J. Edgar Thomson considered it crucial that his company have a way into the South to tap its commercial markets, because the line to Washington was barely pulling a profit.[1]

If Washington was the doorway to the South, then Richmond was its core, with railroads expanding to every part of the state and the region. The State of Virginia, as early as the year 1830, saw the prospects in a rail line linking the two capitals of Richmond and Washington. In those days, a journey from Richmond to Washington via horse and wagon along Virginia's badly maintained roads averaged three days of travel, and only if the roads were all in good condition, which was a rare occurrence indeed. Travelers needed a more reliable and less tiring route between the two major cities. In 1834, Virginia's General Assembly chartered a railroad called the Richmond, Fredericksburg and Potomac Railroad Company (or RF&P) to build a track to cover half of that distance, from Richmond to Fredericksburg. A few months later in 1835, a company called the Falmouth and Alexandria Railroad Company formed to build the other half of the connection, from Washington to Fredericksburg.

Construction on the RF&P Railroad got underway, but the Falmouth and Alexandria Railroad did not. North of the

Andrew Russell's 1863 photograph shows several men at the construction site of the Potomac Creek bridge in Stafford County on the Richmond, Fredericksburg and Potomac Railroad line.[2]

Aquia Creek in Stafford County, the Potomac River's western shoreline is dotted with many hills and tributary creeks. It would have necessitated massive engineering works to bridge over the deep cut valleys along the river, which was not a financially viable option at the time. By 1842, the RF&P Railroad was up and running from Broad Street Station in Richmond as far as the Potomac Creek estuary at Aquia Creek fourteen miles northeast of Fredericksburg, where passengers and freight would disembark from their trains and take steamboats for the rest of the journey up the Potomac River to Washington. This new railroad shortened the travel time between the cities of Richmond and Washington to approximately fourteen hours.[3]

A second attempt to build the railroad line between Fredericksburg and Alexandria came in March of 1851, when

Virginia's General Assembly chartered a new company called the Alexandria and Fredericksburg Railroad Company. They were to build a spur from the RF&P Railroad line at Brooke Station to the north and west via the Occoquan River to a connection with the Orange and Alexandria Railroad and the Manassas Gap Railroad at Manassas Junction (the route highlighted by the dotted white line on the adjacent map). The new company would have accomplished a roundabout route between Fredericksburg and Alexandria detouring around the rugged terrain along the Potomac River shoreline. Unfortunately, financial woes doomed its construction.

Five years later in 1856, a third attempt came when the Virginia General Assembly turned over the project to the RF&P Railroad. They thought an addition to an existing line would be useful to both railroads, and they even sent out survey crews to prepare a route along the Potomac River. However, the breakout of hostilities in the Civil War in 1861 caused the attempt to fail. The RF&P Railroad became a prime target of both the Union and Confederate armies throughout the war. It provided the only direct route for Union troops to reach Richmond, the Confederate capital.

The cities of Alexandria and Fredericksburg are only forty miles apart, as the crow flies. Yet at the time of the Civil War, the only connecting all-rail route between the two cities required a passenger to travel over four times that distance. Starting in Fredericksburg, a passenger would take an RF&P train thirty miles south from Fredericksburg down to the town of Hanover Junction. From there, a second train runs west for fifty miles along the Virginia Central Railroad to the

This map shows existing railroad lines in Virginia in 1852. The solid white line traces the circuitous route of travel between Fredericksburg and Alexandria by rail. The dotted white line shows the route the Alexandria and Fredericksburg Railroad proposed to build from Aquia Landing to Manassas Junction to avoid the difficult terrain along the Potomac River.[4]

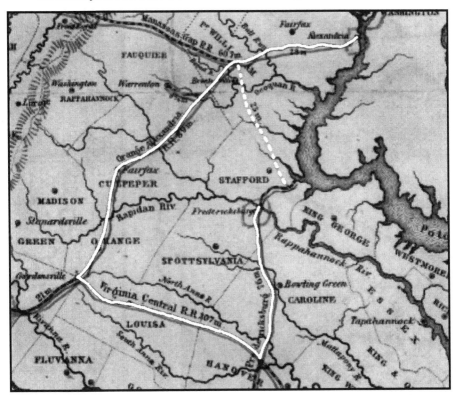

town of Gordonsville. There, yet another train transfer occurs for an eighty mile ride north on the Orange and Alexandria Railroad by way of Manassas Junction into the city of Alexandria. That route, also highlighted on the map above, is so roundabout as to make it ineffective for passenger travel. For that reason, freight and passengers continued to transfer to steamboats at Aquia Landing in Stafford County for the slightly faster fifty-five mile journey up the Potomac River to Washington, D.C. where they could transfer to the Baltimore and Ohio Railroad.[5]

During the height of the Civil War, a fourth initiative to build a route from Alexandria to Aquia was undertaken. Few know that Alexandria was the state capital of Virginia between 1863 and 1865, or at least according to its Union occupiers. The self-proclaimed "Restored Government of Virginia" formed under the leadership of Governor Francis H. Pierpont in 1861 to bring law and order to all areas of Virginia that were under control of the Union armed forces. It quickly earned the recognition of President Abraham Lincoln as the only legitimate government of the entire state. Rather than recognize the Confederate state government in Richmond, Pierpont characterized them as "large numbers of evil-minded persons that have banded together in military organizations with intent to overthrow the Government of the State; and for that purpose have called to their aid like-minded persons from other States, who, in pursuance of such call, have invaded this commonwealth."[6]

Pierpont and his government met in Alexandria at the "official" governor's residence, built in 1804 as the Bank of Potomac Building located today at 415 Prince Street. At the close of 1863, Pierpont met with Union General Daniel McCallum several times. McCallum was the head of the United States Military Railroad, which was in charge of operating any rail lines seized by the Union forces during the Civil War. McCallum brought up the goal of not only controlling existing railroads, but also completing a new direct land route for military supplies to the depot at Aquia Landing and for troops on the march toward Richmond. Pierpont quickly set out to renew the 1851 charter for this railroad company, and approved a five-year extension to the charter on February 3, 1864. Pierpont called it the Alexandria and Fredericksburg Railway Company. Note that the new company name includes the word "railway" and not "railroad" as did the former 1851 company with the same name. In railroading culture, a name change of this type marks the formation of a new corporation that is independent of the old company.[7]

The new charter gave the construction rights to the owners of the Alexandria and Washington Railroad, a convenient arrangement since it was under the control of McCallum and his United States Military Railroad at the time. The true owners of the railroad had joined the Confederate Army only to have their property confiscated by the Union for the war effort and the railroad dubiously sold by Pierpont to northern owners. That railroad ran from the Long Bridge (today's Fourteenth Street Bridge leading over the Potomac River) into the City of Alexandria and saw use throughout the war for moving Union Army supplies to the many depots on the Alexandria waterfront.[8]

The Alexandria and Washington Railroad got the right to expand their line directly south, along the Potomac River, to a link with the RF&P Railroad at Aquia Creek. During the last year of the Civil War, the company was no match for the large engineering project that lay ahead, and the United States military engineers that could have helped complete the project were assigned to more immediate projects during the war. Following the war, the original Southern owners of the railroad returned to Alexandria and quickly filed lawsuits to regain control of their railroad. The company itself remained tied up in court proceedings between the two sets of owners until 1870, well after the five-year charter to build south expired in February of 1869.

Governor Francis Pierpont chartered the Alexandria and Fredericksburg Railway at his residence located at 415 Prince Street in Alexandria. This former Bank of Potomac Building housed the Union state government.[9]

These legal entanglements were not going to slow down Joseph Stewart, the first president of the Alexandria and Fredericksburg Railway. Following the war, Pennsylvania Railroad President John Edgar Thomson and Vice President George Brooke Roberts made several personal visits to Stewart on behalf of their own railroad company in which they pledged the backing of the Pennsylvania Railroad for the new line if the charter was renewed. In March of 1866, Stewart boldly travelled to Richmond to meet the head of the RF&P Railroad, Peter Daniel, Jr. In that meeting, Stewart presented a daring proposal to have the Pennsylvania Railroad finance the building of the Alexandria and Fredericksburg Railway and then buy out the RF&P Railroad. These actions confirmed the worst fears of the owners of the RF&P Railroad at the time, the Robinson family of Philadelphia. The Robinsons were concerned with maintaining their own steamboat line now running a successful operation between towns all along the Chesapeake Bay watershed. They fought the construction of any railroad into Washington to keep this business. For years, the Robinsons had been fearful another railroad company would do just as Stewart proposed.[10]

Initially, monetary support for the Alexandria and Fredericksburg Railway was difficult to gather in Virginia. When Stewart received a lukewarm reception from the RF&P leadership in Richmond, he then travelled to Fredericksburg to drum up support. There, Stewart tried selling stocks to a number of former local government officials and railroad executives. When the railway company issued bonds, barely half of them sold. In the end, Daniel McCallum put his own

The Robinson family wanted to keep their steamboat business between the wharf at Washington, pictured here, and Aquia Creek. The proposed Alexandria and Fredericksburg Railway threatened that business.[11]

funds forward to get the railroad underway. He hired the construction contractors, Bodfish, Mills and Company to start surveying the railroad line out from the City of Alexandria, even though they had no approval from the state government to operate the railroad yet.[12]

In February of 1870, Pennsylvania Railroad leadership persuaded the owners of the Alexandria and Fredericksburg Railway Company to sell their ownership stakes. Now with the full financial backing of the eager President John Edgar Thomson, a lobbying team formed under the leadership of James Seger. Knowing the financial straights that the state government was in following the war, Seger attempted to have the General Assembly pass a bill permitting the

Pennsylvania Railroad to buy a controlling share in any Virginia railroads. In return, the Pennsylvania Railroad would buy out the state's railroad holdings and pay its share of the taxes. It was defeated in the first vote, but Seger kept busy. He purchased advertisements in the local newspapers, wrote editorials and continued meeting with lawmakers. That June, Seger and his team persuaded enough members of the Virginia General Assembly to change their votes and the bill passed. Importantly, an amendment to the bill also reinstated the Alexandria and Fredericksburg Railway's former 1864 charter, and the Pennsylvania Railroad now held the rights to build a railroad line from Alexandria as far south as the town of Quantico.[13]

The Robinson family was livid. Public accusations flew back and forth between the company presidents. The Richmond newspapers of the day eagerly printed every word for then, as today, people loved to gossip. Robinson accused the Alexandria and Fredericksburg Railway of hiding behind the skirts of the northern railroads, and wondered loudly why a second railroad was needed in an area already covered successfully by his own RF&P Railroad for many years. The Pennsylvania Railroad pushed right back and accused the RF&P of sidelining their own railroad so that their steamboats would become more valuable. One of the best quotes came out of the Richmond Times-Dispatch on January 11, 1871, in which Robinson stated that the Alexandria and Fredericksburg Railway attracted, "wild, adventurous and dissolute speculators. I tremble for Virginia, for her purity and her own morals to allow her inside."[14]

Emboldened by these successes, President J. Edgar Thomson believed that his railroad could continue to build or buy his way along friendly lines through Virginia into North Carolina. Not content just to connect to the RF&P Railroad, another bill quickly came before the General Assembly. This bill seemed innocuous enough on the surface, simply asking for permission to change the railroad name from the Alexandria and Fredericksburg Railway to the Washington and Richmond Railway. However, the true purpose of the bill was more nefarious. Buried in the bill was a bid to extend the tracks of the renamed railroad all the way to Richmond and connect with the Richmond and Danville Railroad, another Pennsylvania Railroad subsidiary company. It would bypass the RF&P Railroad. The bill passed through the General Assembly, but lawmakers still loyal to the Robinson family sabotaged the bill by filling it with amendments to make it useless to the Pennsylvania Railroad. The Pennsylvania Railroad then chose not to accept the legislation.

Chapter Three
FIRING THE LOCOMOTIVES

ℰⴹ

"I have been all over the United States, but this is the first railroad I ever saw tied to a tree."
– Phineas Barnum

ℰⴹ

With a vision and a plan in 1871, Pennsylvania Railroad President J. Edgar Thomson moved quickly to begin construction on the Alexandria and Fredericksburg Railway. Beginning in the south in Lorton and travelling north into the city of Alexandria, the following pages will be a journey along the new railroad right-of-way in Fairfax County to visit the stations and flag stops along the line and meet the landowners whose property the Alexandria and Fredericksburg Railway would cross.

Doctor Thomas Nevitt had his property condemned for the railroad right-of-way and a station called Telegraph Road. The station house was located on the west side of the track approximately 800 feet south of Lorton Road on Gunston Cove Road. Born in 1806, Dr. Nevitt was successful in nearly every venture het set upon. His farm in Lorton brought in a steady income for his wife and several children. He served as a Justice of the Fairfax County Court for 25 years before the Civil War broke out. He licensed as a physician early in the war and quickly became one of the most respected doctors in the county, opening a large practice in Washington after the hostilities ended. Doctor Thomas Nevitt passed on in 1875 at the age of 69. His gravesite is located in the Pohick Church cemetery.[1]

The station gained its name from the road that ran through his property. Route 642, today known as Lorton Road, has an older history. Earlier called Telegraph Road, it saw use as a service road for the first public telegraph line

Thomas Nevitt Street is located in the Gunston Square subdivision in Lorton.[2]

built in the state of Virginia. The Washington – New Orleans Telegraph Company erected the telegraph here in 1847. This particular section stretched from the District of Columbia south to Petersburg, Virginia.[3]

This line played a vitally important role as one of only two telegraph trunk lines that served the South at the outbreak of the Civil War in 1861. Both sides during the conflict sought to destroy each other's modes of communication, and routinely targeted this telegraph line during raids. Some sections of this route still exist as Telegraph Road throughout the South. The roadside marker for the telegraph is located at Pohick Church.[4]

Lucy Fowler also had property condemned for the railroad right-of-way and two stops named Pohick and Accotink. Ms. Lucy Fowler is the daughter of John Fowler, who owned a plantation on the north side of Pohick Road and earned a living as a land surveyor for Fairfax County following the Revolutionary War.

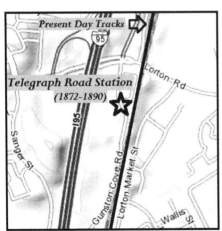

Left: The location of Telegraph Road Station from 1872 to 1890.[5]
Right: The roadside marker for the telegraph line located at Pohick Church.[6]

The Pohick stop consisted of just a small waiting shelter located on the western side of the track approximately 400 feet southwest of the current Virginia Railway Express platform at Lorton Station. The Pohick stop gained its name from nearby Pohick Creek, a fourteen-mile-long stream running from Burke to Fort Belvoir. The word "Pohick" is a Native American term meaning "hickory" that comes from the Doeg people. They lived along the watersheds of the Potomac River in southeast Fairfax County.[7]

Accotink Stop also featured a waiting shelter located on the eastern side of the track, approximately 200 feet south of Pohick Road where it crosses the railroad tracks. Today it is a commercial storage site. Accotink Stop got its name from nearby Accotink Creek, a stream running for twenty-five miles through the heart of Fairfax County. The name "Accotink" is an Algonquin Indian term for "at the end of the hill."[8]

Richard L. Nevitt deeded over twelve acres of land for the railroad right-of-way and a station called Long Branch. The

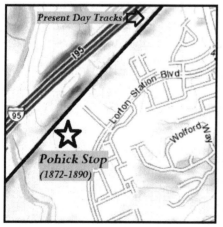

Left: The location of Pohick Stop from 1872 to 1890.[9]
Right: The location of Accotink Station from 1872 to 1890.[10]

Long Branch is a tributary creek of Accotink Creek leading from Fort Belvoir to Franconia that crossed his property in a north to south alignment. Long Branch Station was located on the eastern side of the track, and the track ran along what is today Cinder Bed Road. Today, the station site is approximately 200 feet north of the intersection of Newington Road and Cinder Bed Road; just yards away from the creek that bears its name.[11]

Richard Nevitt was born in 1824 in Maryland to parents William and Rebecca Nevitt. Richard Nevitt was the owner of the Newington house in 1872 when the railroad came through his property. Originally, his home was a Church of England rectory house completed in 1760 for the Truro Parish. It gained the name of Newington after it became the private home of Richard and Sarah McCarty Chichester after 1767. The Nevitt family acquired the house and 1,000 acre tract in 1828. Richard Nevitt was a private in the Sixth Virginia Cavalry during the American Civil War, and occupied

Left: The location of Long Branch Station from 1872 to 1890.[12]
Right: The Newington roadside marker on Newington Road.[13]

the house with his wife until it burned down in April of 1875. Oral history stated that it was the oldest house standing in Fairfax County at the time. Today the roadside marker for the station stands at the entrance to Levelle Dupell Park on Newington Road. The private family cemetery is nearby.[14]

On February 20, 1871, Anna Maria Fitzhugh (shown in the painting below) had nineteen acres of land condemned for the railroad right-of-way. Her property would host a waiting shelter called Ravenworth. Oral history claims that the letter "S" dropped from the name Ravenworth to differentiate this railway stop from Ravensworth Station already in existence on the Orange and Alexandria Railroad near the town of Annandale. The waiting shelter was located on the western side of the track on the Cinder Bed Road pathway found directly to the west of what is today Amberleigh Park. The concrete foundation may still survive. Access at the time was by a path leading from Back Lick Road through what is today the Loisdale Estates neighborhood.

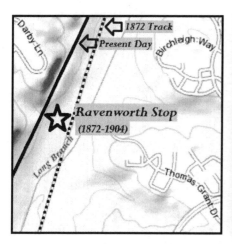 

Left: The location of Ravenworth Stop from 1872 to 1904.[15]
Right: A painting of Anna Maria Fitzhugh, the owner of Ravensworth.[16]

Anna Maria Sarah Goldsborough Fitzhugh was born in 1796 to parents Charles and Elizabeth Goldsborough of Maryland. Her father was a longtime member of Congress and Governor of Maryland. Anna Maria married William Henry Fitzhugh in 1814, an only son and principal heir to the Ravensworth land grant. The name Ravensworth honors the family's ancestral estate in England, the seat of the Barons of Ravensworth. At age 38 in May of 1830, he died suddenly and unexpectedly of a stroke while visiting Anna Maria's father in Maryland. Dying without an heir since they had no children, his wife was left the Ravensworth mansion in Springfield (shown in the photograph below) and 11,000 acres of land covering what is today Springfield south of Braddock Road. Anna Maria passed away in 1874. The home survived until it mysteriously burned down in 1926.[17]

Richard Windsor had three acres of land condemned on February 20, 1871 for the railroad right-of-way. His property would host a flag stop named Windsor. The waiting shelter

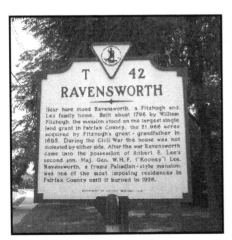 

Left: The roadside marker for the Ravensworth mansion.[18]
Right: A photograph of the rebuilt mansion, ca. 1940.[19]

was located on the southern side of the track approximately 800 feet east of the present-day Franconia-Springfield train platform. The old roadbed cut is still visible near the Franconia-Springfield Parkway overpass. Access to the stop was by paths leading through the present-day Windsor Estates and Springfield Forest neighborhoods.

Richard Windsor was the proprietor of the Hayfield Plantation between 1860 and 1874. The property name comes from George Washington, who originally acquired the property in 1761 and used it to grow hay. Following his return from the Revolutionary War, he sold the property to his cousin and Mount Vernon plantation manager, Lund Washington, who built the Hayfield manor house and outbuildings on the property.[20]

The house, shown in the photograph below, stood on the corner of what are today Hayfield Road and Bing Court until it burned down in a fire in 1917. Hayfield owner William Clarke was responsible in 1874 for building the double-

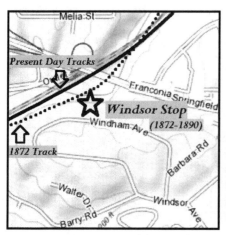

Left: The location of Windsor Stop from 1872 to 1890.[21]
Right: A photograph of the Hayfield mansion house.[22]

octagon (sixteen-sided) barn. It was a replica of the one built by George Washington, and remained a community fixture until it too burned down in a 1967 arson fire.

Robert Rollins Fowle had six acres condemned by the railroad company on January 20, 1871, but also deeded over another twelve acres on October 18 of the same year to the railroad in exchange for a station named Franconia. The name Franconia originated from his father, William Fowle's 191-acre Frankhonia Farm located near today's Franconia volunteer fire station. William Fowle originally purchased this land from Joseph Broders of neighboring Oak Grove. Robert Fowle was born in 1832 and educated at Harvard. During the American Civil War, he operated in several different Confederate units including the Sixth Virginia Cavalry, Kemper's Alexandria Artillery and the Second Virginia Cavalry. After the war, he married Barbara Sanders and managed the Frankhonia Farm from his home on Potter's Lane near Old Franconia Road until his death in 1873.[23]

Left: The location of Franconia Station from 1872 to 1903.[24]
Right: The roadside history marker for Franconia Station.[25]

Franconia Station was located on the eastern side of the track approximately 800 feet south of Franconia Road across from present-day Fleet Drive near Trips Way in the Greenwood subdivision. The station house was actually a converted family home. The first floor played host to the railroad office and the Garfield Post Office in its early years, while the second floor housed the family of a railroad worker, normally the head of that section of the railroad. The roadside history marker about the station, shown in the photograph on the previous page, is located in the parking lot of the Franconia Governmental Center on Franconia Road.

On April 20, 1871, the railroad company condemned nineteen acres of land from Francis M. Gunnell for the railroad right-of-way and a stop called Bush Hill. Bush Hill was not a regular flag stop, but did see use by the Gunnell family. The Bush Hill stop was located on the south side of the tracks, north of what is today Eisenhower Avenue. "The Exchange at Van Dorn" condominiums stand today just to

Left: The location of the Bush Hill Stop from 1872 to 1905.[26]
Right: A photograph of the Bush Hill house ca. 1950.[27]

the south, where historical markers relate the history of the Bush Hill home. Access to the stop and the Gunnell farm was via Bush Hill Drive.

The name "Bush Hill" comes from the Gunnell family ancestral home in England, but the Bush Hill home here has a history all its own. Built in 1763 by Alexandria merchant Josiah Watson, it was a beautiful example of Georgian architecture. Union General Oliver O. Howard used the home as his headquarters following the First Battle of Manassas in 1861, and the federal government leased the property in October of 1942 to house Hitler's defected counselor of foreign affairs, Ernst "Putzi" Hanfstaengl during the Second World War. The home, shown in the photograph on the previous page, burned down in 1977.[28]

It was near Holmes Run, bordering today's Ben Brenman Dog Park that the Alexandria and Fredericksburg Railway would intersect with the Virginia Midland Railway, formerly known as the Orange and Alexandria Railroad. Railroading

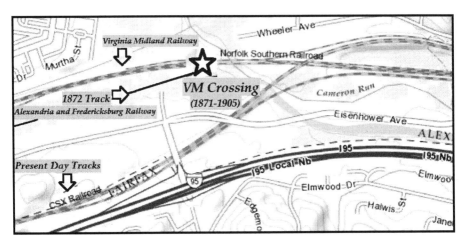

At "VM Crossing" the Alexandria and Fredericksburg Railway crossed southwest to northeast, while Virginia Midland Railway crossed northwest to southeast.[29]

tradition holds that when a railroad company crosses a pre-existing railroad line, the newcomer is required to build and maintain that crossing. In this case, the Alexandria and Fredericksburg Railway built a small structure in August of 1871 to house a telegraph operator and a signalman to make sure that the trains of the two railroads did not attempt to use the intersection at the same time and collide. It would be named the VM Crossing (for Virginia Midland), but the call sign on the telegraph wire would be "AF" for Alexandria-Fredericksburg since they would be managing the trains at the crossing. The crossing would serve until 1905, when the realignment of the tracks moved the crossing further east. The building itself saw use as a storage shed until after the Second World War, when it was finally demolished.

On May 20, 1871, D. F. Forrest of the neighboring Clermont Plantation had two acres of his land condemned for the railroad right-of-way and a stop called Seminary. There was no shelter or train siding here, only a cinder platform.

Left: The location of Seminary Stop from 1872 to 1890.[30]
Right: A photograph of the seminary's chapel ca. 1900.[31]

Those waiting for a train could not wait by the track, but instead had to wait out on the roadway. The platform was located on the south side of the railroad track at the end of Quaker Lane in Alexandria. At the time, a road ran between the Burgundy farm in the south and the Virginia Protestant Episcopal Theological Seminary located about one mile to the north, hence the name of the stop.

Bishop William Meade, the Bishop of Virginia and Francis Scott Key, the author of "The Star-Spangled Banner," founded the seminary in 1823 to educate men for religious service. That first year, they had fourteen students enrolled and just two professors to teach them. During the American Civil War, the buildings at the seminary served as a field hospital for nearly 2,000 wounded Union soldiers, 500 of whom did not leave the seminary grounds. The seminary reopened after the war, and they built the chapel shown in the photograph on the previous page in 1881. While the beloved chapel burned down in 2010, the seminary continues educating students to this day.[32]

With the Alexandria and Fredericksburg Railway close to completing its line to Quantico, the stockholders of the RF&P Railroad authorized building a ten-mile extension of its line leading from Brooke Station in Stafford County in order to join with the tracks of the Alexandria and Fredericksburg Railway at a new wharf on Quantico Creek. The RF&P Railroad completed that extension, only to find it was nearly two miles short of the town of Quantico. Since the stockholders charter specifically imposed a ten-mile limit, the only option was to allow another company to finish their line.

A look back at the Alexandria and Fredericksburg Railway...

Below left: A roadside history marker explains that the original 1872 rails belonging to the Alexandria and Fredericksburg Railway were unearthed during the construction of the Asher building in the year 2012.[33]

Below right: The rails underwent restoration and now run along the brick sidewalk next to the Bastille Restaurant. They are located on the west side of North Fayette Street between Pendleton and Wythe Street in Alexandria.[34]

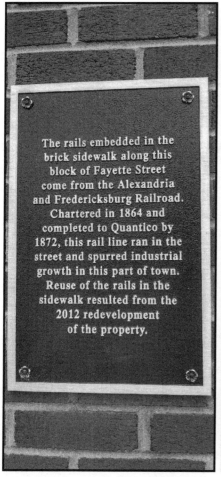

The rails embedded in the brick sidewalk along this block of Fayette Street come from the Alexandria and Fredericksburg Railroad. Chartered in 1864 and completed to Quantico by 1872, this rail line ran in the street and spurred industrial growth in this part of town. Reuse of the rails in the sidewalk resulted from the 2012 redevelopment of the property.

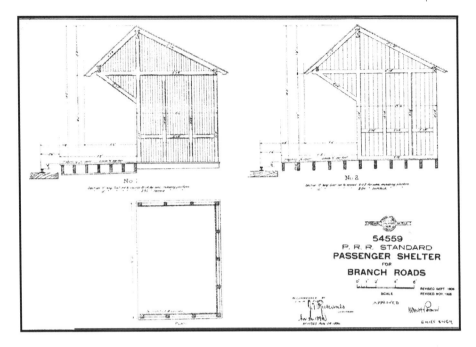

Above: A blueprint of the standard passenger shelter erected at every stop along the Pennsylvania Railroad, including those on the Alexandria and Fredericksburg Railway.[35] **Below:** Richmond, Fredericksburg and Potomac Railroad engine 307 at Franconia Station. Note the Pennsylvania Railroad's standard passenger shelter to the right of the train.[36]

In came a subsidiary of the RF&P Railroad called the Potomac Railroad Company, who built a 1.7-mile-long rail line to span the town of Quantico and connect the two railroads together. It completed the work on May 1, 1872, and then agreed to lease the line to the RF&P Railroad.

Two months later on July 2, the Pennsylvania Railroad work crews completed the 27-mile single-track Alexandria and Fredericksburg Railway line. This made possible, for the first time, a direct passenger route between Philadelphia and North Carolina. As a subsidiary company itself, the Alexandria and Fredericksburg Railway did not own any locomotives or rail cars of its own stock; the Pennsylvania Railroad was its sole operator. Their crews worked the trains between Alexandria and Quantico where they changed over to RF&P Railroad crews and engines for the rest of the journey to Richmond.[37]

105

ALEXANDRIA & FREDERICKSBURG R. W.

Number.	NAME.	Dist. fr'm Quantico.
1	Quantico (Junc. R., F. & P. R. R.)†	
2	Quantico (North Side of Creek)	0.6
6	Cherry Hill	3.9
8	Freestone	5.9
	Negley*	8.4
	Mount Pleasant*	9.3
14	Woodbridge†	10.7
18	Telegraph Road	13.8
19	Pohick	14.3
20	Accotink	14.8
23	Long Branch	17.0
25	Ravenworth	18.4
27	Windsor	19.5
28	Franconia	20.5
	Bush Hill*	23.7
	Seminary*	24.8
37	Junc. Virginia Midland Railway	27.3
38	Alexandria (Engine-House)	27.3
40	Alexandria†	27.5
	St. Asaph Junction (A. & W. R. R.)*†	29.0

The Pennsylvania Railroad Stations and Sidings Guide from 1884 lists the distances between stops along its new line.[38]

The Pennsylvania Railroad now had rail lines leading south through Washington to the Long Bridge on the Potomac River, and its new Alexandria and Fredericksburg Railway line running north into Alexandria. Just seven miles of track operated by the Alexandria and Washington Railroad Company was all the Pennsylvania Railroad was lacking for sole control of a rail route between Philadelphia and Quantico. Through a series of legally dubious maneuvers, the Pennsylvania Railroad acquired a portion of the Alexandria and Washington Railroad's right-of-way for their own use. They pushed the Alexandria and Washington Railroad near bankruptcy by building a track paralleling their existing line less than thirty feet away. The Pennsylvania Railroad then purchased a controlling interest in the company at basement prices and merged it into its own system.[39]

With the Alexandria and Fredericksburg Railway now complete, residents in Fairfax County certainly had reason to be confident in the future. Just owning property in the general vicinity of the railroad line through Fairfax County caused land values to quadruple. Local newspapers of the day reported that the new railroad would make Fairfax County one the greatest agricultural producers in the entire state. This pronouncement proved true, and many dairy farms in the Franconia neighborhood were able to run very successful operations into the twentieth century.

Of course, the Fairfax County Board of Supervisors was not about to let a source of taxable income just wander past them. Perceiving a chance to take advantage of the deep pockets of owners far off in Philadelphia, the Board of

Supervisors more than tripled the amount of taxes levied on railroad equipment and land within the first decade of the railroad's operation. Unfortunately, this tax came back to hurt the county in the form of drastic reductions in service. The neighboring Washington and Ohio Railroad even went to the county court to receive a ruling against the county treasurer to prevent him from collecting on those taxes. The county supervisors then backed down and restored taxes back to pre-construction levels.[40]

The death of visionary Pennsylvania Railroad President John Edgar Thomson hit the company hard in 1874, just as the Alexandria and Fredericksburg Railway was going into full service. The man to take over operations as the new head of the line was Thomson's right hand man and former Vice President of the Pennsylvania Railroad, Thomas Alexander Scott. Scott was born in 1823 in Fort Loudon, Pennsylvania. Early on, work was important to Scott. He was educated in country schools during the wintertime while he worked on a farm the rest of the year. Though his education was limited, Scott continually educated himself through reading books.[41]

In 1850, the Pennsylvania Railroad hired Scott (pictured here) to work as a station agent.[42] At that time, they were building railroads all over the country. Those who were good at making decisions, like Scott, could move up the company ladder quickly because of the need for managers. During the American

Civil War, Scott thrived as the Assistant Secretary of War and was in charge of all of the Union government's railroads and means of transport, including all of the telegraph lines. He became intimately familiar with the Alexandria area during this time. In fact, he named the headquarters of the United States Military Railroad on Cameron Street the "Scott House."

When Scott took over as president of the Pennsylvania Railroad in 1874, he was now in charge of the largest railroad in the world under one management. He was in a position of such immense power that when people from Pennsylvania spoke of "the President," they needed to clarify if they were speaking about Scott or about the President of the United States. Scott would guide the Alexandria and Fredericksburg Railway for the next six years.

On June 1, 1880, Scott retired from the Pennsylvania Railroad. He died on May 21, 1881, at his home located near Darby, Pennsylvania. Some believed that he worked himself to death. Back on the new railroad though, Thomas A. Scott had a lot to deal with. Quickly and poorly constructed as a winding and hilly railroad, the original 1872 track laid for the Alexandria and Fredericksburg Railway was not located exactly where the railroad line is today (that change occurred between 1903 and 1907), but took a slightly different route.

One might logically expect the railroad to follow the path of today's Route 1 or Interstate 95 that people know so well. However, it does not. In fact, from the Potomac River all the way into Quantico, it is very tough to get alongside the tracks. Regrettably, the railroad and highway planners did not concur on where to put their rights of way, so the roads and tracks do not even remotely parallel each other. The railroad goes around harbors and houses, slices through woodlands and farms, hops over and under roadways, slithers between hills and in short does everything except parallel the roads. The term "tree tunnel" might best describe most of the path.

Leaving the City of Alexandria in a westward direction, the track ran near today's Eisenhower Avenue paralleling the Virginia Midland Railway tracks to the south until reaching Holmes Run. Near today's Ben Brenman Park, the train dispatcher at CR Tower watched over an at-grade crossing of those two railroads. Continuing west, the track passed over today's Van Dorn Street. Nearing Backlick Run and Valley View Drive, a difficult series of winding twists and turns sent the tracks southward at a higher elevation until passing today's Franconia-Springfield Station, where the tracks followed the course of Cinder Bed Road past Newington. There the tracks followed their present-day course through the towns of Lorton and Colchester until crossing over the Occoquan River into Prince William County.

The Alexandria and Fredericksburg Railway had sections of the line constructed over oily marine clay that permitted the tracks to shift after the passing of every train. In colonial times, local farmers reported this legendary Virginia red clay to have the ability to swallow up entire roadways overnight without leaving a trace. That constantly shifting rail bed would be responsible for several train derailments over the years, even up to one hundred years later. In one act of amazing desperation, railroad workers tore apart most of the old wooden Long Bridge leading over the Potomac River into

Washington and used the lumber from it in an attempt to shore up the sides of the roadbed.[43]

Maintaining a moderate grade along the railroad was not easy given all the hills and valleys along the route. Cuts through hills required shoring up dirt and clay, lest a landslide occur. In 1872, the Alexandria Gazette reported at one of these landslides that a temporary wooden bridge was constructed and ropes secured the bridge to trees further up the hill while crews repaired the tracks. It delayed many trains including the famous Ringling Brothers Barnum and Bailey Circus Train. Delayed by the incident on the way to Fredericksburg, Phineas Barnum commented that he had been all over the United States, but this was the first railroad he had ever seen tied to a tree.[44]

This photograph by Herbert French shows the Long Bridge in 1865 following the American Civil War. Note the older Long Bridge standing to the right in the photograph. The Pennsylvania Railroad repurposed the lumber from that bridge to shore up the railroad bed.[45]

This photograph is of a train climbing the Franconia Grade on the Alexandria and Fredericksburg Railway. Note the deep, fresh cuts in the rock that were distinctive features of the cuttings near the Forrest family property.[46]

Other problems faced were not so easily resolved. In the early years of the railroad's operation, just a decade after the Civil War and during the height of Reconstruction, many Virginians deeply resented the Pennsylvania Railroad's northern influence in the line. They performed small acts of sabotage and, in one case, even attempted to remove spikes and rails from the track in order to trap a locomotive stopped at Alexandria. In addition, worker safety was always a concern around trains in the early years. In 1872, John Walker was working for the railroad company on the construction of the High Bridge over the Occoquan River when he fell seventy feet to his death on the rocks below. In

1876, flagman Michael Grimes attempted to get off a train while in motion at Franconia Station and had his toes crushed. In addition, engine No. 89 instantly killed Richard Roberts while he drove across the tracks in 1884 near the Seminary Stop.

Another problem would never go away: in a geological oddity, Franconia Road would be located at the peak of a five-mile-long hill located at 250 feet above sea level, the highest point on the entire railroad line between Washington and Richmond. For perspective, Alexandria's Union Station is only thirty feet above sea level. The average gradient is approximately 0.8 percent ascending southbound into Franconia Station from the current-day Telegraph Road overpass and 0.6 percent ascending northbound into the station from Pohick Creek.

Named the "Franconia Hill" or the "Franconia Grade," the steep grade is a major obstacle to freight train operations, even into the present day. Freight trains will crawl up the hill at less than fifteen miles per hour, resulting in a transit time up the hill in excess of twenty to thirty minutes. This includes the time it takes the rear of a long freight train to clear the hill, and reduces valuable track capacity. If a train stalled on the hill, the crew could wait for a push from another train or they could cut the train into two halves and take the front end to the next siding, then return for the rest of the cars.

Bitterness from the local populace subsided over time, as did the inconsistencies in the track bed. However, there were also other railroad companies ready to step in should the Pennsylvania Railroad fail in its new endeavor. President

Thomas Scott had two major competitors in his quest to establish and maintain a profitable railroad in Virginia. The first competitor was the Baltimore and Ohio Railroad lead by John Garrett. Their battle was over the Long Bridge, the only bridge trains could use to cross over the Potomac River into the city of Washington.

The Baltimore and Ohio Railroad held a monopoly on railroad traffic in the District of Columbia until the Pennsylvania Railroad came along in 1869. Through a subsidiary called the Baltimore and Potomac Railroad, the Pennsylvania Railroad managed to build a railroad line into Washington and gain control of the Long Bridge. The only option left for Garrett was to send trains all the way to Harper's Ferry to cross into Virginia. Having lost the railroad bridge over the Potomac River, Garrett decided instead to start a ferry for train cars at Shepherd's Landing in Maryland. The landing was located at the southern point of what is today Joint Base Anacostia–Bolling, just inside the District of Columbia line.

Completed in 1874, the ferry brought train cars across the Potomac River right to the foot of Wilkes Street in Alexandria. Thus, the Baltimore and Ohio Railroad bypassed the Pennsylvania Railroad's blockade of the Potomac River. The ferry only lasted a couple years before the Baltimore and Ohio Railroad realized the ferry service was slow and unreliable. The two competing railroads finally came to an agreement in 1876, in which the Alexandria and Fredericksburg Railway would transport rail cars for the Baltimore and Ohio Railroad if they paid a per-car fee.

Train cars are loaded onto a barge to be ferried down the river.[47]

Over the long term, the second competitor to the Pennsylvania Railroad was the larger issue. The Pennsylvania Railroad had a very touchy relationship with John Robinson and his Richmond, Fredericksburg and Potomac Railroad to the south. Each company now controlled half of the route between Washington and Richmond. They relied on each other, yet neither company wanted to be under the thumb of the other. John Robinson had little interest in helping the rival Pennsylvania Railroad operate a train on his tracks while his steamboat service was still successful in his eyes and initially allowed only a single late-night passenger train to continue all the way from Washington to Richmond. Passengers who wanted to travel by daylight still had to use steamships for the Potomac River journey to the wharf at Quantico.[48]

The stubbornness of the RF&P Railroad leaders certainly hurt the Alexandria and Fredericksburg Railway. President Scott reported that it operated at a $10,000 loss for the first year since the two companies could not agree on how to transport freight across each other's lines. For nearly a decade, the two railroads continued escalating their efforts to outmaneuver each other. Both companies brought no less than five bills before the Virginia General Assembly in those years to gain approval to build a railroad line to bypass their competitor. It finally came to a climax in 1881, when Pennsylvania Railroad executives threatened to bypass and completely abandon their own Alexandria and Fredericksburg Railway in order to starve the RF&P Railroad of revenue opportunities. The public itself also greatly preferred an all-rail trip to transferring to steamboats. The RF&P Railroad finally backed down and shuttered its steamboat service. Thereafter, the two rivals cooperated more closely with one another. By the beginning of the twentieth century, railway travel had become a reliable conduit between Washington and Richmond.

Chapter Four
WASHINGTON SOUTHERN

ℬ ℭ

"Don't let the train of enthusiasm
run through the station so fast that
people can't get on board."
– H. V. Morton

ℬ ℭ

With the retirement of Pennsylvania Railroad President Thomas A. Scott in 1880, the Alexandria and Fredericksburg Railway was now in need of a new leader, and George Brooke Roberts was just the person. Born in 1833 in Bala Cynwyd, Pennsylvania, he started working for the Pennsylvania Railroad at the age of nineteen. Many of the colleagues of George Roberts acclaimed him as one of the best business minds to work at the railroad, being reasonable and honest in his deals. Roberts is to thank for securing the purchase of the

Alexandria and Fredericksburg Railway a decade earlier. As Vice President, he personally oversaw most of the design, construction and early management of that railway, so he knew its intricacies well.

Ascending to the presidency of the railroad in 1880, Roberts greatly expanded the company. He invested more than fifty million dollars in rails and equipment, more than all the previous presidents combined. By the end of his sixteen-year term as president, the Pennsylvania Railroad was the biggest private employer in the United States and the biggest corporation in the world. The old saying, "behind every successful man is a good woman" is true in the case of George Roberts and his wife Sarah. She was responsible for the naming of several train stations before she died in childbirth in 1868. George Roberts himself died in Philadelphia in 1897 after sixteen years at the helm.

Pennsylvania Railroad President
George Brooke Roberts (1833-1897)[1]

George Brooke Roberts was responsible for bringing the Alexandria and Fredericksburg Railway into a new era. Trouble over the acquisition of the Alexandria and Washington Railroad a decade earlier was coming back to bite them. In 1879, the court in Alexandria began to question how the Pennsylvania Railroad was able to acquire its land. The case continued up the judicial ladder, including going before Virginia's Supreme Court and the United States Circuit Court, with each court reversing the ruling of the courts below it.

The final decision came five years later in 1884, when the court ordered the Pennsylvania Railroad to pay a small compensation to the Alexandria and Washington Railroad and ordered it sold at foreclosure. This meant little, since the Pennsylvania Railroad had ownership over both companies by that time. Per the courts request, the Alexandria and Washington Railroad's land sold at auction in June of 1887 for a quarter of its net worth. The buyer was one Francis Smith, an attorney for the Pennsylvania Railroad, who immediately sold the land right back to his employer. On January 20, 1890, the Virginia General Assembly authorized the merger of the Alexandria and Fredericksburg Railway with the bankrupted Alexandria and Washington Railroad.[2]

The new company would go by the name of the Washington Southern Railway Company and run service on an expanded 33-mile route from Washington to Quantico. Effective April 1, 1890, the Washington Southern acquired all property and rights of the two predecessor corporations. The Pennsylvania Railroad would still control and operate the

Washington Southern Railway for eleven more years, but big changes were on the way.

One notable change under the new management team was that Telegraph Road Station would receive a name change to Lorton Station. The station house itself would not move, but the new name reflected the changing character and growth of the surrounding neighborhood. Joseph Plaskett was the man responsible for the name Lorton. He immigrated to the United States from his hometown in Cumberland County, England named Lorton Valley. When he became the first area postmaster in 1875, he named his new post office Lorton Valley to commemorate his former home. Generations of the Plaskett family also served as postmasters at Lorton until the post office closed in 1910. The post office was located at the intersection of Gunston Cove Road and Richmond Highway, less than one mile from the railroad station.

Prior to the construction of Shirley Highway through the middle of Lorton, it was a small but thriving community. The

Left: A photograph of Lorton Station from across the tracks.[3]
Right: The location of Lorton Station from 1890 to 1971.[4]

Lorton School started in 1878, and the current brick building dates to 1934. The village of Lorton also played host to general stores operated by the Springman and Tillinghast families, a blacksmith shop and even an attempt at a telephone exchange service. Today, Joseph Plaskett still resides near his beloved home in the Lewis Chapel cemetery. There is a roadside marker erected at the entrance to Lorton Station Town Center to commemorate the Plaskett role in forming the Lorton community. The photograph on the previous page shows the Lorton station house.

Also, Long Branch Station had a name change to Accotink Station to honor the nearby town surrounded by Fort Belvoir on Richmond Highway. It is easy to drive past this little village, and yet, it is so much more than just a shortcut from Fort Belvoir to the Fairfax County Parkway. It was a thriving community in the early nineteenth century founded by the large Quaker community living there before the military condemned all the land around it.

Left: The location of Accotink Station from 1890 to 1904.[5]
Right: Accotink Church still stands in the center of the village.[6]

Accotink had a schoolhouse, general store and post office. Its residents were lawyers, carpenters and doctors. While over-farming depleted the soil, the sale of timber was a lifeline for families with large plots of forested land. The gristmill and shipyard on Accotink Bay were big industries. Today, few hints of this history remain, and the town spans only a single block. The biggest reminders remaining of that history are the 1880 Accotink Methodist Church (shown in the photograph on the previous page) and cemetery still standing at the center of the community, both listed on the Fairfax County Inventory of Historic Sites.

While those name changes made sense, others were not so easy to understand. One kindly railroad worker accused the Washington Southern officers of "tossing names in the air to see where they would land." To summarize a complicated explanation, for the next thirteen years between 1890 and 1903, there would be three stops using the name Pohick at the same time within one mile of each other on the line. The

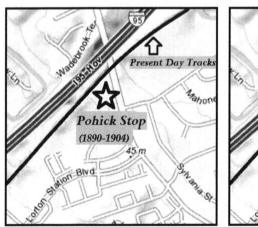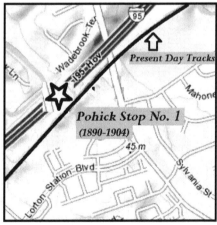

Left: The location of Pohick Stop from 1890 to 1904.[7]
Right: The location of Pohick Stop No. 1 from 1890 to 1904.[8]

Pennsylvania Railroad took the step of listing them all as Pohick, Pohick No. 1 and Pohick No. 2 on their timetables.

The original Accotink Stop located on Accotink Creek would receive a name change to Pohick Stop, due to the Long Branch Station name change. The railroad company chose to expand Pohick Stop by building a shelter for a signalman and a large water tower about 800 feet south of the original stop, and both stops would now go by the name of Pohick. While the northern platform remained the access point for passengers, the southern platform was for freight trains taking on water or coal along with instructions from the signalman prior to the climb up the grueling Franconia Grade. A memorandum from the railroad company archives in Richmond stated that they did not want two stations with the same name in order to prevent confusion, and yet the station located just a half-mile south already had the name Pohick for the past eighteen years. That station would now get the designation of Pohick Stop No. 2.

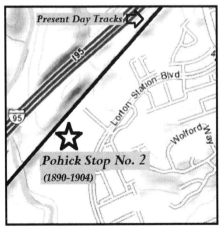 

Left: The location of Pohick Stop No. 2 from 1890 to 1904.[9]
Right: The location of Franconia's Gravel Pit Siding from 1890 to 1903.[10]

Further north, service to the Windsor flag stop ended after only eighteen years of service due to a lack of passenger traffic. The growth of nearby Franconia Station is likely the cause. In 1890, Franconia Station would expand its services to include a second location a half-mile north of the station house. It would feature just a small industrial siding to serve the gravel pit operations that were occurring in the area of today's Franconia District Park. Gravel pits were quickly becoming a feature of the surrounding neighborhood. Gravel from Franconia would see use in the construction of many local roadways and airports. The siding was located on the eastern side of the track approximately 800 feet north of Franconia Road across from what is today Marcy Court.

Another flag stop to appear under the new Washington Southern management was Burgundy. Burgundy Stop derives its name from the home built in 1808 by James Hooe (pronounced HOH), shown in the photograph below. The home stood on a hill just to the south of the private school

Left: The location of Burgundy Stop from 1890 to 1942.[11]
Right: The Burgundy mansion, shown here circa 1910.[12]

that still bears its name. Ownership of the Burgundy farm was in the hands of Thomas Walsh at the time the railroad came through his property.

Walsh came to America in 1840 from Limerick, Ireland. A true immigrant success story, he was a humble apprentice before starting a grocery in Brooklyn, marrying in 1851 and raising ten children. They moved to Burgundy in 1869. Burgundy Road originally served as a driveway leading from Telegraph Road to the mansion house. Fire destroyed the home on the evening of October 15, 1916. Burgundy Farm Country Day School, the first desegregated school in the state of Virginia, has educated students on the property since 1946. Burgundy Stop was located on the south side of the railroad track near what is today the parking lot for Lake Cook, a four-acre man-made lake in Cameron Regional Park in Alexandria. Access to the stop was by Cox's Lane, a small path running between what is today Wheeler Avenue and the Burgundy property.

With the Washington Southern Railway now restructured to the satisfaction of President George Roberts, he found himself becoming increasingly involved in a new state government project in Virginia. Formed in 1893, the Office of Public Roads Inquires was tasked with two seemingly impossible goals. Called the "Good Roads Movement," state officials first needed to overcome the widespread hatred of roads by state residents, and more importantly, needed to educate the public why instituting a new road tax was important for improving the quality of the roads. George Roberts was anxious to see good roads leading to his railroad

This sidings guide shows the Washington Southern stops for the year 1900.[13]

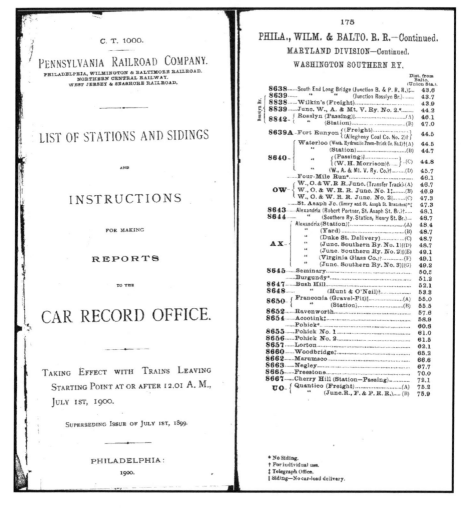

C. T. 1000.

PENNSYLVANIA RAILROAD COMPANY.

PHILADELPHIA, WILMINGTON & BALTIMORE RAILROAD.
NORTHERN CENTRAL RAILWAY.
WEST JERSEY & SEASHORE RAILROAD.

LIST OF STATIONS AND SIDINGS

AND

INSTRUCTIONS

FOR MAKING

REPORTS

TO THE

CAR RECORD OFFICE.

TAKING EFFECT WITH TRAINS LEAVING
STARTING POINT AT OR AFTER 12.01 A. M.,
JULY 1ST, 1900.

SUPERSEDING ISSUE OF JULY 1ST, 1899.

PHILADELPHIA:
1900.

175

PHILA., WILM. & BALTO. R. R.—Continued.

MARYLAND DIVISION—Continued.

WASHINGTON SOUTHERN RY.

		Dist. from Balto. (Union Sta.).
8638	South End Long Bridge (Junction B. & P. R. R.){	43.6
8639	" " (Junction Rosslyn Br.)	43.7
8838	Wilkin's (Freight)	43.9
8839	Junc. W., A. & Mt. V. Ry. No. 2.*	44.2
8842 {	Rosslyn (Passing){............(A)	46.1
	" (Station)................(B)	47.0
8639A	Fort Runyon {(Freight)........} {(Allegheny Coal Co. No. 2)†}	44.5
8640 {	Waterloo (Wash. Hydraulic Press-Brick Co. No.1)†(A)	44.5
	" (Station)..................(B)	44.7
	" {(Passing)†.........} {(W. H. Morrison)†. ..}–(C)	44.8
	" (W., A. & Mt. V. Ry. Co.)†........(D)	45.7
	Four-Mile Run*	46.1
OW {	W., O.& W. R. R. Junc. (Transfer Track)‡(A)	46.7
	W., O. & W. R. R. Junc. No. 1‡........(B)	46.9
	W., O. & W. R. R. Junc. No. 2‡........(C)	47.3
	St. Asaph Jc. (Henry and St. Asaph St. Branches)*‡	47.3
8643	Alexandria (Robert Portner, St. Asaph St. Br.)†...	48.1
8644	" (Southern Ry. Station, Henry St. Br.)...	48.7
AX {	Alexandria (Station)†.................(A)	48.4
	" (Yard).................(B)	48.7
	" (Duke St. Delivery).......(C)	48.7
	" (Junc. Southern Ry. No. 1)‡(D)	48.7
	" (Junc. Southern Ry. No. 2)‡(E)	49.1
	" (Virginia Glass Co.)†.......(F)	49.1
	" (Junc. Southern Ry. No. 3)‡(G)	49.2
8645	Seminary	50.5
	Burgundy*	51.3
8647	Bush Hill	52.1
8648	" (Hunt & O'Neil)†	53.3
8650 {	Franconia (Gravel-Pit)‡.............(A)	55.0
	" (Station)..................(B)	55.5
8652	Ravensworth	57.6
8654	Accotink‡	58.9
	Pohick*	60.8
8655	Pohick No. 1	61.0
8656	Pohick No. 2	61.5
8657	Lorton	63.1
8660	Woodbridge‡	65.2
8662	Marumsco	66.6
8663	Negley	67.7
8665	Freestone	70.0
8667	Cherry Hill (Station—Passing)†	72.1
UO {	Quantico (Freight)................(A)	75.2
	" (Junc.R., F. & P. R. R.)...(B)	75.9

* No Siding.
† For individual use.
‡ Telegraph Office.
‖ Siding—No car-load delivery.

stops so that more passengers and industry could use his line. He supported the government project wholeheartedly. He directed the Washington Southern Railway to donate machinery for road building and even contracted out their own engineering experts to help with planning roads. Thus, the railroad itself had a very active role in promoting a mode of transportation that later became their chief competitor and caused the demise of their business in both freight and passenger traffic.

Following the death of Pennsylvania Railroad President George Brooke Roberts, two leaders would shepherd the Washington Southern Railway into the twentieth century. They were Frank Thomson and Alexander J. Cassatt. Frank Thomson would lead the Washington Southern for two years between 1897 and 1899. He was born in Chambersburg, Pennsylvania in 1841. By the age of seventeen, he was already an apprentice in the railroad machine shops in Altoona and studied mechanical engineering there. Thomson gained experience repairing machinery, rebuilding bridges and constructing new roads and telegraph lines.

Later in life, the press would comment that he could both build a locomotive and act as its engineer. He enlisted in the Union Army during the Civil War, and served as an assistant to Thomas A. Scott, the future leader of the Pennsylvania Railroad. As assistant to Scott, Thomson built railroads and bridges as well as directed the transport of troops and supplies. Thomson joined the Pennsylvania Railroad in 1874, and became President in 1897. Thomson brought two big contributions to the Washington Southern Railway. He was the first to institute a system of track safety inspections, and was instrumental in standardizing the tracks and roadbed used all across the Pennsylvania Railroad system. He died on June 5, 1899, in Merion, Pennsylvania after battling an illness.[14]

A. J. Cassatt would then lead the Washington Southern for two years, between 1899 and 1901. He was born in 1839 in Pittsburgh, Pennsylvania. Cassatt joined the Pennsylvania

Railroad in 1861 as an engineer and rapidly rose through the ranks to become President in 1899. Cassatt made big investments in the Washington Southern. He more than doubled the company's assets during his presidency and led improvements to almost every part of the system. Cassatt pushed for increases in track and equipment spending. The great accomplishment under his stewardship was the planning and construction of tunnels under the Hudson River to bring the Pennsylvania Railroad into New York. Unfortunately, Cassatt died before his grand Pennsylvania Station in New York City was completed.[15]

Alexander Cassatt would be the last Pennsylvania Railroad president to manage the Washington Southern. Near the end of the nineteenth century, the Pennsylvania Railroad had overreached in its attempts to expand into western and southern states in pursuit of a transcontinental railroad. In the midst of an economic depression, stockholders led an

FRANK THOMSON
PRESIDENT PENNSYLVANIA RAILROAD

Left: Frank Thomson, president of the railroad from 1897 to 1899.[16]
Right: Alexander J. Cassatt, president from 1899 to 1901.[17]

uprising and demanded that the company avoid funding any more expansion projects. Pennsylvania Railroad management took that mandate a step further and sold off nearly all of its subsidiary rail lines south of the Mason–Dixon Line.

Showing just how important Southern rail traffic still was to the Pennsylvania Railroad, they could not justify completely cutting ties with the Washington Southern Railway. On November 1, 1901, the Pennsylvania Railroad relinquished its sole control over the Washington Southern and turned over operational control of the railroad to the officers of the Richmond, Fredericksburg and Potomac Railroad Company. The RF&P Railroad now operated 113 miles of track between the capitals of Washington and Richmond in what they dubbed the "Richmond-Washington Line." This change reflected the fact that most rail traffic on the Washington Southern was not local freight destined for rural Fairfax County, but long-distance traffic passing through to serve all the states along the eastern seaboard.[18]

The Richmond-Washington Company incorporated on September 5, 1901 as a holding company, owning both the RF&P Railroad and the Washington Southern Railway. Under the terms of the new agreement, the six railroads connecting to the RF&P Railroad and the Washington Southern Railway owned the entire stock of the holding company in equal parts. Three of those railroads connected with the RF&P Railroad at Richmond. They included the Chesapeake and Ohio Railway, the Atlantic Coast Line Railroad and the Seaboard Air Line Railroad. The other three railroads connected with the Washington Southern Railway in

Washington. They included the Pennsylvania Railroad, the Baltimore and Ohio Railroad and the Southern Railway. The traffic of those six railroads would be handled along the new line between Richmond and Washington with "equal promptness and upon equal terms." The Richmond-Washington Company became essentially a bridge line serving its owning railroads, and thus the Pennsylvania Railroad still had access to markets in the South. Although the Washington Southern Railway now had a new owner and operator, it would continue to keep its name and its company records independent from those of the RF&P Railroad for another nineteen years. Train crews, however, would operate between Richmond and Washington without stopping to change out company employees and engines in Quantico, as had been standard procedure in the past.[19]

Even Virginia's state government wanted to defend this new rail line. When state legislators drafted a new state constitution in the year 1902, they created the State Corporation Commission. This agency would be in charge of regulating the railroads and other public works projects. In the past, the creation of a railroad required the direct approval of the General Assembly, but now they gave that power to the State Corporation Commission. However, the drafters of the new constitution purposely gave the General Assembly the right to "prevent, by statute, the construction of any railroad parallel to the RF&P line." Quickly taking advantage of this provision, the General Assembly passed an act, effective May 21, 1903. It provided that: "No railroad company chartered under this Act or whose character may be amended under this

The cover of this railroad timetable from 1912 depicts the "Richmond-Washington Line." The joining of the Washington Southern Railway with the Richmond, Fredericksburg and Potomac Railroad occurred in 1901.[20]

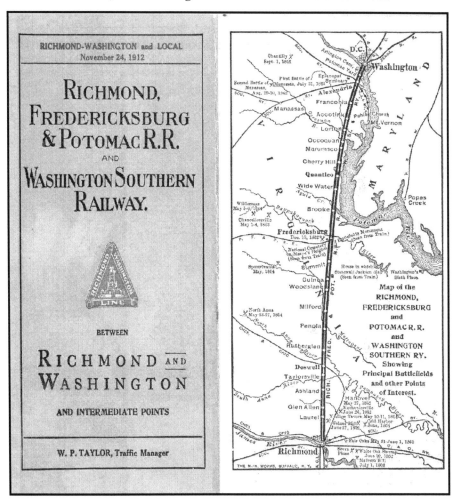

Act shall have the power to build any railroad parallel to the line of the Richmond, Fredericksburg and Potomac Railroad."[21]

An unforeseen side effect of this new arrangement was a staggering increase in the traffic that passed through the City of Alexandria. At the switching yard located near today's

Holland Lane, hundreds of rail cars routinely backed up for a mile through the city streets of today's Carlyle neighborhood next to the National Cemetery.[22] The Washington Southern needed a new rail yard built to handle and sort the traffic for all the railroads that now owned the company and wanted to send their freight through Washington. Completed in 1906 just north of the city, it went by the name of Potomac Yard and featured a very complex set of railroad tracks for sorting, loading and storing freight cars. It would become one of the busiest rail yards on the American East Coast in the years to come.[23]

Chapter Five

RAILROAD REALIGNMENT

ℬℭ

"Rail travel at high speeds is not possible because passengers, unable to breathe, would die of asphyxia."
– Dionysius Lardner

ℬℭ

Freight traffic over the new Richmond-Washington Line increased quickly, and the train dispatchers running the show from Richmond found that the single track they had was inadequate for the number of trains they wanted to run. The number of trains allowed on a single track at the same time is severely limited because trains cannot run too close to each other without risking a collision. For this reason, they added a second track along the entire line between Richmond and Washington in a process called "double tracking." They also realigned the tracks onto the course they follow to the present day during this four-year construction project between 1903 and 1907. They eliminated or smoothed out sharp curves and reduced hills in grade, including lowering the peak of Franconia Hill underneath Franconia Road by a staggering twenty feet. They put almost the entire line of track in a new location between Quantico and Alexandria, all in an effort to speed up transit times along the line.

Not all went smoothly during the double tracking operations. A terrific explosion occurred near Franconia Road that shook houses for miles, blew out glass from windowpanes and spooked residents who heard it as far away as Arlington and Fairfax City. At 1:30 in the morning on Saturday, May 21, 1904, a railroad contractor working for Lane Brothers and Jones was carrying a lighted lamp as he walked into a shed where a large quantity of gasoline and dynamite was stored. As he entered, the flame from the lamp ignited the gasoline fumes, which flared up all around him.

ALEXANDRIA AFFAIRS

TERRIFIC EXPLOSION STARTLES RESIDENTS OF FRANCONIA.

The Detonation Heard Seven Miles Away—No One Injured—General and Personal.

Special Correspondence of The Evening Star,
ALEXANDRIA, Va., May 21, 1904.

The Evening Star on May 21, 1904 headlines the surprising event of the day.[1]

He immediately turned and ran out the door. His escape was not a moment too soon, as the dynamite went off with a mighty explosion reducing the small building to splinters. No injuries occurred in the contractor's camp, as the shed was thankfully located at some distance from the sleeping workers. Many residents stated it to be the largest explosion ever to hit Fairfax County, but other residents also remembered the deadly explosion of the gunpowder bunker at Fort Lyon in the Huntington neighborhood forty years earlier.[2]

In addition, a lawsuit arising from the track work for the Washington Southern Railway would go before the Supreme Court of the District of Columbia. On the evening of November 29, 1904, an Irish contractor named Dominico Glaria was departing his worksite at Franconia Station. The home that he shared with several other Irish railroad workers lay a mile to the west near what is today Robert E. Lee High School in Springfield. It was a foggy evening, and a large dirt embankment blocked Glaria's view of the tracks. When he stepped onto the track to walk across, passing express train No. 403 ran over his leg. Doctors in Alexandria were unable to save his leg, which required amputation above the knee. Glaria claimed the train was travelling above the speed limit when he was crossing over the track and did not receive any warning from the train.[3] His lawsuit accused the railroad company of negligence and asked for reparations of $25,000 for his personal injuries. Taking into account inflation over time, that is the equivalent of over a half million dollars today. The court initially ruled in favor of Mr. Glaria, but later overturned the decision on appeal in the year 1908.[4]

During this large construction project, the Washington Southern Railway would purchase or condemn land along the new right-of-way in order to realign the tracks. In Fairfax County, the railroad company completed the realignment and double tracking in two distinct segments. They rebuilt the track running in a north/south alignment between Franconia and the Occoquan River in 1904 and 1905, and the track running in an east/west alignment between Franconia and Alexandria City in 1905 and 1906. Also important to note is that the two miles of track operated by the Potomac Railroad in Quantico transferred to the Washington Southern Railway in 1904. The RF&P held the lease on that segment of the railroad for 32 years.

The survey crews for the Washington Southern Railway had a large task ahead of them to plot a new course for the railroad. These men were trekking through miles of fields, forests and streams to plot the fastest path a train could take. The survey crew would put stakes in the ground tied with ribbons to show the direction they wanted the tracks to go. Those same crews later used survey instruments to obtain exact measurements. They documented the property the railroad company needed to purchase, or who to take to court in condemnation proceedings if they chose not to sell. All aboard! Beginning in the south in Lorton and travelling north into the city of Alexandria, the following pages will be a journey along the railroad right-of-way to visit the new stops on the Washington Southern Railway.

In 1904, the town of Colchester would receive a new flag stop. The station would be located on the eastern side of the tracks where the former Ox Road (now Furnace Road) crosses under the train tracks. In 1753, Colchester was the first town established in Fairfax County. It prospered for a few years as a trading center and tobacco port. However, silting in the river and a change away from tobacco as a primary crop doomed Colchester as a port town. The final nail came when the state built a bridge across the Occoquan River bypassing Colchester for its more prosperous neighbor, the Town of Occoquan. The railroad stop lasted for fifty years. Today, only a single private home, the Fairfax Arms, shown in the photograph below, remains as a reminder of this colonial era community.

The first stops to suffer abandonment under the new management team would be two of the three stations named Pohick. The sole survivor would be the station house and water tower located on the south side of Pohick Road. The reason for this selection comes back to its location at the base of Franconia Hill. It was the last chance for northbound

Left: The location of Colchester Stop from 1904 to 1953.[5]
Right: The Colchester Inn is the oldest standing structure in town.[6]

steam engines to take on water so that locomotives could make the grueling five-mile climb without stalling, and the first station for southbound trains to recover at after descending the hill.

Accotink Station also relocated a quarter-mile northwest to its new location where today the tracks cross Newington Road in an office park. The original concrete underpass still stands at only twelve feet wide and fifteen feet high to allow local traffic to pass under the railroad. The station would become the focal point of the surrounding community, with Pearson's general store and Newington post office as neighbors for many years to come.

The decision came not to relocate the Ravenworth waiting shelter on the new rail line. Two factors played a role in that decision. First, the platform and rails were prone to frequent flooding from the Long Branch stream located just feet away. Secondly, its location on the north-south Back Lick Road doomed the stop, since freight traffic was primarily coming

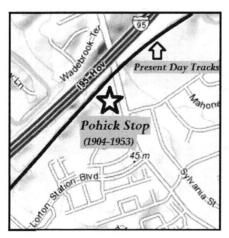 

Left: The location of Pohick Stop from 1904 to 1953.[7]
Right: The location of Accotink Station from 1904 to 1954.[8]

from the west to the east on the Old Fairfax Pike, now known as Franconia Road. The railroad company wanted to focus on the stations nearby at Accotink and Franconia that sat at these important east-west crossroads. However, the important South Franconia interlock and an industrial siding also bearing the name Ravensworth would soon come to take its place. The Ravenworth shelter had been in service for 31 years.

As noted earlier, Franconia Station was a two-story frame house that had served as part railroad depot and part family home for the Hutchinson family. The home burned to the ground in an accidental fire in December of 1903, although the family did make it out safely. A new station house, shown in the photograph below, was quickly built a half-mile north of its original location on a site that, conveniently, already came with a prepared siding used to serve the area's numerous gravel pit operations.[9]

The station house was located on the eastern side of the track approximately 800 feet north of Franconia Road across

Left: The location of Franconia Station from 1904 to 1953.[10]
Right: The Franconia station house stood for nearly fifty years.[11]

from what is today Marcy Court. Franconia Station would greatly expand its presence there to house an animal pen, small freight house, telegraph office and several railroad worker homes and sheds for equipment. It also would feature a thriving "team track," an extra spur line that the railroad company would park boxcars on for the public to use. It saw use by farmers and merchants in the Franconia area who could personally load or unload items that had arrived by train and deliver them to locals.

Moving ahead to 1905, the Lunt flag stop opened on Old Lincolnia Road. Samuel H. Lunt (1846–1925) started out working as a pharmacist in Alexandria with his father and brother before branching into real estate speculation at the turn of the twentieth century. The photograph below shows the family home downtown at 631 King Street. The Lunt waiting shelter was located on the south side of the tracks roughly 200 feet west of South Van Dorn Street, located on what is today a used car lot.

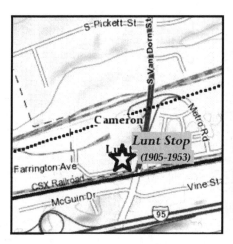 

Left: The location of Lunt Stop from 1905 to 1971.[12]
Right: The Lunt family home today at 631 King Street.[13]

Samuel Lunt arranged many of the land transactions and condemnations throughout the Alexandria area for the railroad. When he lobbied for a flag stop to serve property he wanted to develop, the railroad company was happy to oblige. It would serve the local community for another 70 years, and remained useful when they constructed a new spur for warehouses. The station platform remained in place until 1985 when a new Van Dorn Street underpass for the Capital Beltway necessitated the destruction of the old platform.

The Bush Hill flag stop also relocated onto the new Washington Southern rail line. It moved a quarter-mile south of its original location onto the north side of the tracks where today "The Exchange at Van Dorn" condominiums stand. Official service to the flag stop temporarily ended when the federal government began leasing Bush Hill to house Adolf Hitler's defected counselor of foreign affairs, Ernst "Putzi" Hanfstaengl during the Second World War. Following the war, the stop operated again for a couple years before the

Left: The location of Bush Hill Stop from 1905 to 1946.[14]
Right: A waiting shelter was built at Seminary Stop in 1905.[15]

death of Bush Hill owner Leonard Gunnell in 1946. At that point, rail service ended to the historic property when the surviving family members divided the property and sold portions to developers. The stop had served the family for eighty years. Just a couple years later, a small commercial spur would again carry the name "Bush Hill" for the warehouses located on Eisenhower Avenue where the home stood.

Also improved in 1906 was the stop at Seminary. The stop had been a dangerous and uncomfortable one for passengers due to a lack of shelter against the rain or wind, as well as the need to cross other railroad tracks to reach the train. In 1906, the waiting platform moved to the north side of the tracks, and the Washington Southern installed a shelter for passengers to wait in at the foot of Quaker Lane. Simple measures like these were a nod to the success the Washington Southern had in improving train safety. Also during this time, improvements were made around Seminary Stop to speed up the sorting of traffic coming into the city from the south.

During the realignment of the railroad, they also focused on places where roads crossed the tracks. In an effort to minimize at-grade crossings and keep trains moving, the railroad company erected a series of traffic underpasses and bridges. For example, the photograph on the next page shows the bridge leading Bush Hill Drive over the railroad tracks to serve the Bush Hill farmhouse and saw use until construction of the National Capital Beltway. Nearby, a tunnel stood on Clermont Drive to allow the Forrest family living on the nearby Clermont property a road to pass under the railroad. It was a concrete structure twelve feet wide and

This bridge led Bush Hill Drive over the railroad until construction of the Beltway.[16]

fifteen feet high. This road and the underpass existed until construction in 1985 brought a new four-lane underpass of the Capital Beltway to Eisenhower Avenue.[17]

The largest single feat of engineering undertaken by the railroad company in Fairfax County was the construction of the Occoquan High Bridge in 1872. Rebuilt in 1915, it spans 920 feet across the Occoquan River at a height of seventy feet above the water to avoid the need for a drawbridge.[18] Known as a "Parker through truss bridge" after its designer Charles H. Parker, the truss design is a common feature of railroad bridges built in the late nineteenth and early twentieth centuries. A Parker bridge is distinct in that when viewing the bridge from the side, the triangles forming the superstructure appear in the shape of a camel's hump. Some bridges of this type remain scattered through Maryland, but their numbers are dropping rapidly as newer bridges take their place.[19]

The original 1872 and rebuilt 1892 railroad bridge were not wide enough to accommodate the two tracks the Washington Southern wanted, so the celebrated engineer Gustav Lindenthal rebuilt the Occoquan High Bridge two years before designing his most memorable bridge, the Pennsylvania Railroad's Hell Gate Bridge in New York City. Lindenthal loved public art sculptures and wanted his bridges not only to serve their purpose of ferrying people and trains, but also to serve as a work of public art for the community, pleasing to view. In working on the Occoquan High Bridge, Lindenthal had the mighty Phoenix Iron Company behind him. Phoenix Iron started in 1783 near Philadelphia, Pennsylvania and would remain one of the most prolific bridge builders in the country even 200 years later.[20]

The true testament to the quality workmanship and design of the bridge was when Hurricane Agnes hit in 1972. The High

Engineer Gustav Lindenthal rebuilt the Washington Southern Railway's High Bridge over the Occoquan River in 1915.[21]

Bridge survived the worst natural disaster to hit Fairfax County in the twentieth century, while the two neighboring bridges carrying vehicular traffic across the Occoquan River were badly damaged (in the case of the Route 1 bridge) or destroyed altogether (in the case of the historic Route 123 bridge). The Occoquan High Bridge is on the Fairfax County Inventory of Historic Sites.

Another important bridge looks over the former at-grade crossing of Franconia Road at the tracks next to Franconia Station. Due to the curving track and steep embankments, it was a dangerous crossing where trains would often fly through with little or no warning. It took the deaths of four people at this crossing for Fairfax County to realize the importance of installing a wooden bridge here in 1905, and replacing it with a more modern steel bridge in 1918.[22]

RF&P Railroad Engine No. 502 cresting the top of Franconia Hill at milepost 99.0 underneath the Franconia Road Bridge built in the year 1918.[23]

Especially heartbreaking is the story of the Gorham family of Franconia. On the afternoon of October 13, 1904, Mary Gorham was walking back home from a day's work in the Moore family cornfield. Her son, Samuel, was walking with her when he suffered an epileptic seizure causing him to step out onto the tracks in front of a speeding locomotive at Franconia Station. In an incredible act of bravery, Mary Gorham sacrificed her own life for her son by pushing him out of the path of the oncoming train. She was 69 years old at the time.[24]

Chapter Six

"I Am Not in Denial!"

*"The light you see at the end of the tunnel
is the front of an oncoming train."*
- David Lee Roth

In the beginning, steam locomotives were only capable of speeds under thirty miles per hour, but as time went on, they became faster and more widespread. The Pennsylvania Railroad system was one of the safest railroads in the country in comparison to its competitors of the day. Still, bringing a fully loaded train barreling at eighty miles per hour to a complete halt became a tricky challenge for engineers. Railroads would not install expensive signal devices and safety systems to prevent crashes until the Interstate Commerce

Listed below are those who died in Fairfax County on the Alexandria and Fredericksburg Railway and its successor railroads prior to the year 1980. The author acknowledges that this is not a complete list.

Died	Name	Age	Burial
3/20/1872	John T. Walker	29	Powcan, VA
8/4/1873	Michael Sullivan	8	Savannah, GA
2/21/1877	Elizabeth Penn	82	Cynthiana, OH
10/6/1877	William Henderson	42	Leesburg, VA
2/26/1878	W. C. Mainwaring	24	Baltimore, MD
2/26/1878	John W. Aldridge	41	Fredericksburg, VA
5/19/1882	William Campbell	37	Woodstock, VA
9/13/1884	Richard F. Roberts	70	Alexandria, VA
8/1/1889	Jeremiah Desmond	41	Alexandria, VA
7/10/1899	John K. Nevitt[1]	42	Lorton, VA
2/16/1903	Walter Wiggington	15	Richmond, VA
3/14/1903	John Purvis	23	Shipman, VA
10/13/1904	Mary Gorham	69	Franconia, VA
11/14/1916	Osie Rogers[2]	18	Franconia, VA
10/4/1919	William Armstrong	30	Portsmouth, VA
5/4/1923	Wallace Hopkins[3]	21	Stuart, VA
2/19/1951	Edgar Washington	56	Arcadia, VA
9/27/1957	Victor P. Hammer	53	Altoona, PA
5/20/1969	Eugene S. Drayton	58	Alexandria, VA
1/20/1970	Clara Fleming	74	Goldsboro, NC
1/20/1970	Eva Witherspoon	58	Baltimore, MD
10/2/1979	John W. Boggs[4]	52	Rochester, PA

Commission passed federal guidelines ordering it in 1930.

Yet, more trains were continuing to cross each other's rail lines. There were many procedures in place to prevent crashes, yet catastrophe still occurred. However, the many deaths that have occurred on the railroad should not scare people away from what is normally a safe, reliable and enjoyable transit option. People are more likely to drown, be bit by a shark or killed by a farm animal than to die in a train accident. Now, how is that for a steel lining?

Prior to the double tracking construction project discussed in the previous chapter, the Alexandria and Fredericksburg Railway operated just a single track along its route. Northbound and southbound trains had to share the same track. The number of trains allowed on a single track at the same time is severely limited because trains cannot run too close to each other without risking a collision. Unfortunately, that very scenario occurred at 7:30 in the evening on Thursday, August 1, 1889.[5]

A southbound passenger train had departed from Alexandria's Union Station an hour before under the direction of Conductor Robert E. Murdock and Engineer Jeremiah Desmond. They were under orders to pull over onto the siding at Lorton Station to wait so that a northbound train could pass them on the single track. However, Murdock and Desmond were late in leaving Alexandria, and decided to run the train well above the speed limit in order to make up lost time and still make the siding at Lorton. Even though it was still daylight, a curve in the track south of Pohick Stop meant

The photograph below shows cars of the northbound freight train following the accident. The crews of both locomotives, with the exception of Engineer Desmond, had just enough time to jump away before the collision.[6]

neither train was visible to the other. Murdock and Desmond just a half-mile from pulling into Lorton Station when they met the northbound freight train at full speed. Murdock noticed the impending disaster too late, and could only stare at his watch in confusion and dismay. As all hands aboard leapt from the engine, they called to Desmond to do the same. Not understanding the situation, Desmond exclaimed, "Why?" The crash smashed up both engines and badly wrecked the train cars. The impact threw the tender above the cab and crushed Desmond to death inside. He left behind his wife and seven children in Alexandria. Twenty passengers were also injured in the crash.

If there is a positive aspect to this tragedy, a fortunate last-minute decision did spare more deaths. At Alexandria's

Union Station, the Wheeler family was looking forward to travelling home to Woodbridge after a day in the city. When the train pulled in, the three young Wheeler children eagerly boarded the first car of the train. Just prior to departure, they all switched to the rear car of the train on a suggestion from the father, sparing them from the devastation the front car sustained in the wreck.

Sometimes, train accidents had nothing to do with the trains. On February 16, 1903, Franconia Station played host to a civil disturbance that turned far from civil. The conductor summoned local police on board to arrest a resident of Franconia, Carl von Wedel, for attacking another Franconian, Lee Gorham on board a Washington Southern train. According to other passengers aboard the train at the time, Gorham had scolded Von Wedel for disturbing the other passengers and an intense argument ensued. Von Wedel struck Gorham several times and knocked him down to the ground. Other passengers intervened to help Gorham, but not before a punch from Von Wedel badly cut his right eye. Doctor Arthur Snowden conducted the operation to remove the eye at Alexandria Hospital. The county court fined Carl Von Wedel $100 over the incident.

Franconia Station also played host to one of the most daring train robberies to hit the American east coast. The train involved was the "Florida Flyer," the Atlantic Coast Line's train number 61 running regular service from New York City to Jacksonville, Florida. At approximately ten o'clock on Thursday evening, February 18, 1915, two masked men boarded the train while it was in motion southbound at

Alexandria's Potomac Yard. They clung to an iron step and guardrail that attach to the side of the express car and rode along there. After passing Lunt Stop near South Van Dorn Street, the two men gained entry to the express car by breaking through the glass window of the car doors on both ends. The men threatened the manager of the car, A. Y. Chambliss, with revolvers if he did not open the door for them to enter.[7]

Chambliss yelled out loudly for his assistant, M. M. Williams, but Williams had taken ill and was sleeping. Under threat of death, Chambliss opened the car doors at both ends for the men. They overpowered Chambliss and took his revolver and cash from his wallet. Chambliss handed over his keys, but when he offered to open the safe for the robbers, they refused him curtly. When the keys that Chambliss handed over all failed to open the safe, the men instead smashed a toolbox, took out a fire axe and started hacking unsuccessfully at the top of the safe.

Several attempts were made by the men to open the safe, including trying to blow it open with a small amount of explosives. When the safe still withstood all they could throw at it, the masked men picked up the safe, weighing a staggering 200 pounds, and tossed it off the rear of the train while the train was slowing down to arrive at Franconia Station. They locked Chambliss and Williams inside the rail car and made their escape, stealing two cars near the station. The robbery went undiscovered until the train pulled in at the end of the line at Byrd Street Station in Richmond. This was even odder because the train had made its usual layover of

Pictured here is a safe of the same design that was on board the Florida Flyer train. Dynamite was used to blow open the top of this safe.[8]

several minutes in Fredericksburg. In fact, the flagman, W. F. Robertson and the train conductor, James Southward had walked along the length of the train to see that all was well, and they saw no suspicious sign and no cry for help came from the locked express car.

The first sign of trouble came when a Southern Express agent in Richmond went to enter the car to pick up papers from the safe. He found neither Chambliss nor Williams bound or gagged in any way, and wondered why they did not immediately sound an alarm after the robbers had departed the train. The only theory authorities had was that the men, so frightened by the experience, never thought to report it. "I am not in denial," Chambliss supposedly said. Chambliss and Williams gave a hurried statement to Richmond authorities, but the train waits for no one. Chambliss had to finish the express run to Jacksonville, Florida, after which he returned to Washington to assist in the robbery investigation.

The railroad company reported later that the safe was not carrying anything of value at the time of the robbery, just seventeen dollars in cash, a spare revolver and some papers. What the robbers apparently did not know was that large shipments of valuables or deposits for large banks often moved by the morning express train, not the evening one. In fact, the morning express train just twelve hours earlier had carried $73,000 in cash along the same route. The famed Pinkerton National Detective Agency took up the case, suspecting construction workers near Accotink Creek were involved in the heist. However, the authorities never caught the two masked men.

Director General of Railroads Walter D. Hines (1870–1934) believed the government was not responsible in court cases originating on private railroads.[9]

Wrecks will occur in the course of operating a railroad, but the court case of Hines v. Garrett in 1919 sought to hold the Washington Southern Railway legally responsible for failing to provide enough service for one of its passengers. The court case would become a great battle over the meaning of "proximate cause." During the First World War, young women and wives who lived in the country were more often taking trains and trolleys into the big cities to find work to support their families while a large portion of the men who used to hold those jobs were off fighting in Europe. One such woman was eighteen-year-old Julia May Garrett. She lived with her parents near Seminary Stop on Duke Street and commuted daily into Washington for a clerical job with the Southern Railway.[10]

On February 2, 1919, Garrett missed her usual Southern Railway train after work and chose to purchase a ticket on the rival Washington Southern Railway, which also ran a train to Seminary Stop. Unfortunately, Garrett's train missed the stop at Seminary. She demanded the train back up to the station, but train personnel were unhelpful and instead the conductor let her off a mile further down the railroad. The conductor had apparently told her she could get off now or ride the train to the end in Richmond. The area at Cameron Station was a known homeless camp and lawless area at the time. Railroad workers knew the area was trouble, as robbers had attempted to hold up several trains operated by the Washington Southern passing through that area. While she walked the tracks alone back towards her home, Garrett was detained and raped twice, first by a soldier and then by a drifter.[11]

Garrett's lawyers initially sued the railway company for negligence, pain and suffering in the Fairfax County Circuit Court. Since the Washington Southern Railway was under federal control during the First World War, the railroad company claimed that all legal responsibility lay with the government. For that reason, Julia Garrett's lawyers instead sued the United States Director General of Railroads, Walter D. Hines. Hines did his best to discredit Ms. Garrett in court and delayed proceedings and appeals for years. Garrett initially won in the county circuit court, but an appeal made by Hines to the Virginia Supreme Court ended with a remand back to the county court. In the end, Garrett settled outside of court for just three hundred dollars, missing a chance to set a major precedence in law.[12]

One of the more curious accidents on the RF&P Railroad line occurred on September 17, 1932. All rail traffic halted for the day after a fourteen-car train derailed at Accotink Creek. Several of the freight cars were demolished, causing tons of soda and fruit to escape into the creek below. For years afterward, bemused locals would enjoy recalling the day they saw hundreds of apples bobbing their way down the creek toward the Potomac River. None of the train's crew was injured, but that must have been one "sweet" cleanup effort.[13]

Another accident might have been expected on a Sunday instead of on Thursday, July 23, 1942. RF&P Railroad officials said that a "sun kink" caused the Washington to Richmond passenger train called the "The Sun Queen" to derail near Accotink Creek. Track repair crews were working on that very section of track at the time of the accident, but were not at fault. William Aiken, the general superintendent of the RF&P Railroad, explained that severe heat sometimes causes unusual rail expansion, resulting in kinks. The train ran off the tracks at a switch that had kinked, bowing outward by several inches. There were eleven rail cars in the train, and the last car turned over while the two in front ran off the tracks, but remained upright. Nearby Fort Belvoir Hospital treated about 25 passengers for minor injuries.[14]

Not every incident had a horrible ending. In 1943, disaster nearly struck in Franconia but for the heroism of Howard E. Blunt, a 26-year-old RF&P Railroad fireman from Ashland, Virginia. Mr. Blunt prevented a disastrous wreck of the Champion Train carrying passengers from Miami, Florida and saved the life of Joe Hulcher, his engineer. According to the Washington Times-Herald news article:[15]

> *"Blunt crawled blindly through a cab thick with steam and flaming coals as the results of a burst boiler flue. He set the emergency brakes at the cost of badly burned hands. The Washington and New York train ground to a stop on a long grade six miles south of Alexandria. Both Blunt and Hulcher were brought a mile down the track on a hand car and rushed to Alexandria in an ambulance awaiting them. Blunt was released from the hospital after three days, although burns on one hand require it to be carried in a sling."*

The worst rail accident in Franconia's history, shown in the photographs on the following page, occurred on the night of Tuesday, January 20, 1970. The Gulf Coast Special is a train that runs regularly from Jacksonville, Florida to New York City, and carried 125 passengers in ten passenger cars on that fateful night. The oily clay in the roadbed caused a 200-foot section of rails to shift as much as three feet out of place after a strong rainstorm earlier in the evening. The train had just passed under the Capital Beltway and was negotiating a ninety-degree turn north of Valley View Drive when it jumped off the tracks at 12:10 a.m. There was speculation the train was traveling above its maximum speed of 80 miles per hour, but the speed limit in the section of track west of Van Dorn Street is only 65 miles per hour.[16]

The conductor of the train, Edgar L. Vaughn, reported that he was in one of the coach cars when the cars "started bumping on the ties and all of a sudden it lurched over." The last car on the train derailed going around the curve, dragging five other cars off the tracks with it, four coaches and two Pullman cars. The crash injured 54 people and killed three women. The victims were Eva King Witherspoon of Baltimore, Maryland, Mrs. Clara Fleming of Goldsboro, North Carolina and Mrs. Eliza McCray of Trio, South

Left: Looking at the tracks where the train finally halted.[17]
Right: Three of the passenger cars slid down a steep embankment.[18]

Carolina. An inspector for the National Transportation Safety Board said the three women were riding in the first coach car, which flipped on its side. The three women, thrown out of the windows, became pinned beneath the rail car as it scraped along the right-of-way. As the engineers brought the three-engine train to a halt, three of the derailed cars slipped down the 60-foot muddy embankment, knocking down small trees along the way. The inspector blamed poor track maintenance for the wreck.[19]

Firefighters from Alexandria and Fairfax County, including Franconia's own Volunteer Fire Department Company No. 5, had difficulty in reaching the remote crash site in the woods. It was nearly a mile away from any major roadway. Once rescuers and civilian volunteers were on the scene, they found the area around the train to be a nearly impassible quagmire of mud. Initially, the only gear that rescuers could get to the wreck site was what they carried on their own backs. Rescue workers worked through the night

Left: Fires were intentionally set by rescuers for light and warmth.[20]
Right: Rescuers pull trapped passengers from the rail cars.[21]

to cut through the wreckage and free passengers. Paramedics transported injured passengers to hospitals nearby at Alexandria and Fairfax for treatment. The uninjured were offered a free ticket to board another train in Alexandria to continue their trips. Stuart Shumate, the president of the Richmond, Fredericksburg and Potomac Railroad at the time of the wreck, turned away questions from reporters regarding financial damage estimates. The Washington Post quoted Shumate saying, "The real sad thing is that three people were killed. You can always fix up steel."[22]

Chapter Seven

THE WAY THINGS WORK

ॐ ॐ

*"When a man boards a Pennsylvania Railroad
train nowadays he has every reason to feel that
he is just as safe as he is in his own home."*
– Lancaster News

ॐ ॐ

Take a moment to consider the engineering challenge of managing miles of thin ribbons of steel track on the ground. Those rails take an enormous daily beating. For example, the rails change shape, expanding and contracting from fluctuations in the air temperature. In addition, ground movement, vibrations, plant growth and the buildup of water, snow or ice all play a factor. Now keep in mind that while most of the time they are just sitting there unburdened, it is in those few remaining moments that they are supporting trains as heavy as one million pounds. Railroad companies discovered the answer to this engineering challenge two hundred years ago and the process has not changed much.[1]

The process of constructing a railroad bed begins with bare ground, and then adds layers on top. First, there is a solid foundation of sand or concrete. It lifts the tracks high enough so they will not get flooded. On top of the foundation, they place the "ballast," or crushed stones with sharp edges. This ballast allows the ground to shift, lets the rain and snow drain from the track, and stops weeds and other plants from growing and rapidly taking over the track. On top of the stones, they place a procession of wood beams at right angles to the route of the train tracks. Each wood beam, called a cross tie, weighs nearly two hundred pounds and is normally doused in chemicals to protect it against the weather. Dumping loads of more small stones to surround the beams actually locks them into position.[2]

Next, they bring in the steel rails. These used to be 39 feet in length because they were carried to the construction site in 40-foot rail cars and laid on top of the cross ties end to end. They used to connect together by fastening an extra piece of steel across the joint, but welding is the more common technique today. One would think that just nailing them down to the wooden cross ties would work, but the natural expansion and contraction of the rail causes them to move and break. Instead, the rails are attached to the cross ties by clips, which hold them down but allow them to move as they expand or contract.

Good quality track ballast is made of crushed stone. The sharp edges
help the stones interlock with each other and hold everything in place.[3]

The design of the train wheels themselves uniquely keeps
the trains on the tracks. The unique cone shape of the wheels
does this, where the outer edge of the wheel is actually
narrower than the inner edge. Consider the problem of a
train going through a curve to the right, when the outside
wheel has to travel farther than the inside wheel. Because of
the cone shape of the wheels, the wheel on the outside rail
then has the larger part of the wheel on the rail and starts
travelling farther with each revolution. The wheel on the
inside rail has the smaller part on the rail and travels a lesser
distance. This steers a train back towards the middle of the
rail, where both wheels are travelling at the same speed. In
effect, here is a centuries old method that is particularly

successful in moving people and goods thousands of miles, even though nothing is fixed to the ground.[4]

At a variety of places down the length of the track, the rails have switches attached, which allow a train to shift from one track to another. Switches are vital for managing traffic. For example, when two trains are in service on the same track, a switch can allow one train to pull onto to a second track while the faster train passes them. Using a series of switches, a train can shift onto another railroad line, or allow many trains to come and go at a busy freight yard.

A switch consists of a pair of moving rails called "points." They are set where two railroad lines branch off from one. One of the points is always touching a rail, and one is not. The points lock together and constantly move as one unit to make sure this is the case. These movable points give direction to the train wheels. If the left point touches the rail, the train turns onto the right track (as shown below), and if

This photograph of a switch shows the pair of tapered moving rails called points.[5]

the right point touches the rail, the train takes the left track. A simple lever switches the points from one position to the other. Early on, a track worker on the ground would be responsible for setting the lever in the correct position before the train came through, a difficult and dangerous job.

As more trains ran along the same track, rigorous control over the rail traffic was needed. Railroads installed signals along the track at strategic intervals as a means of quickly communicating with trains at speed to keep train operators knowledgeable of the conditions ahead. Signals control trains much like traffic lights control cars on roads. The first railroad signals came of age in 1872 at the same time as the construction of the Alexandria and Fredericksburg Railway.

Blocks were another major breakthrough in early train safety. A blocking system divides a line of track into little sections, each managed with signals. Within each block, a signal emplacement protects a segment of the track along with a person to operate the signal. While one train finished passing through a designated block, another train halted at the signal for the block to clear. Then, when everything cleared in the block, the signal changed to show that the way was open and the train carried on its journey.

The big catalyst in signal improvement was the brainchild of William Robinson. The emergence of dependable electricity led to his creation of a railroad signal that made use of the basic principles of conductivity. A box called a "relay" was placed at each end of a block. The box contained circuits and electromagnets. A current from the box electrified each rail. At the end of each block, a narrow piece of insulating material between the rails made sure that the next block could have its own electric circuit and not mess up the circuits of other nearby blocks.

When a train passes into an electric block, the electric circuit from one of the rails will pass across the steel axles of the train to the other rail and create an electric connection. The relay box at the end of the rail then detects this loss of electricity and a series of magnets become demagnetized. This action creates a new electric circuit that then sends power to a railroad signal that rotates a lens in the signal from green to red. That is how electric blocks started, and are still used today. The leader in their manufacture was the Union Switch and Signal Company created by George Westinghouse in Swissvale, Pennsylvania in 1881, and the Washington Southern Railway used these blocks.

The AF interlocking tower was located near the Telegraph Road overpass.[6]

Some areas have more than one train track, with some tracks going in all different directions, places such as yards, crossings with other railroads, or high traffic areas. These were places where manned signals remained a necessity. The railroad company installed manned "interlocking towers" at these spots. Each tower operator was in charge of controlling all the switches by hand and telegraphing the train dispatcher when the train had passed their tower. A two-letter code distinguished each individual tower in a telegraph communication. The letters typically related to the name of the nearby town or station and prearranged so they could not be confused with other letter codes used in telegraph messages. For example, the tower located near the Telegraph Road overpass south of Alexandria controlled the trains running to and from Fredericksburg. The letters "AF," which stood for Alexandria to Fredericksburg, indentified the tower.

Before these towers were prevalent along the railroad, a signalman would be required to physically set each signal and switch to the desired indication by hand. Under the old method of train dispatching, those people whose job it was to schedule and coordinate all the trains had to rely on reports from each individual signalman or telegraph operator to know the location of the trains out on their section of the track. The Alexandria and Fredericksburg Railway sometimes required trains to stop and collect written orders from a stationmaster in person. Not only was this an extremely slow process, it was also very expensive to the company's bottom line. It did not take railroad companies long to recognize that managing a series of signals from one central location would improve the effectiveness of workers and trains.

The first interlocking towers used levers. Simply raising or lowering those levers altered the warning given out by the signals, and changed the corresponding switch on the track. Usually, these levers had some type of prearranged color-coding to let the operator inside the tower know which warning the signal would display depending on which way the lever pointed. Interestingly, these hand-controlled levers stayed in use all the way through the end of the twentieth century in some locations. The interlocking mechanism itself was in fact an early type of computer. The creative design of the interlocking machine permits the tower operator to control a group of levers, setting the train routes in advance,

The Union Switch and Signal Company designed the interlock mechanisms.[7]

without actually allowing a route that would cause an accident. Once a train entered a block, the interlocking machine locked in the set of switches ahead of it, and the machine would not let another train pass through those blocks. A tower operator could order the train to stop in an emergency, but the train's course was set such that the operator could not alter it until the train had completely passed through the block. This "approach lock" especially protected high-speed trains passing through that could not stop quickly. The railroad company designed and built each interlock device exactly for the section of track it would control.

Another interesting feature of the railroad interlocking towers was in their construction. They installed the interlocking machine on site first, and then built the frame of the tower building around the interlock mechanism. They built interlocking towers as two-story buildings due to the immense size and intricacy of the machine parts. The machine normally was located on the first floor of the building, along with a furnace and storage spaces. An outside stairway lead to the second floor, where the operator and switches were located and it featured wide windows looking towards the tracks in every direction for optimal viewing.

There were two main interlocking towers controlling the tracks through Fairfax County. GS Block, later known as CW Tower, stood on the north side of Pohick Creek. The building, shown in the photograph on the next page, remained in operation until 1949. The second tower was AF Tower in Alexandria, located near the Telegraph Road overpass. It operated between 1906 and 1921 in a wooden building, then fifty more years in a brick building on the same site. From the beginning, AF Tower had responsibility over a unique joining of the Southern Railway and the Washington Southern Railway. The designation of "VM Crossing" as the telegraph call sign referred to the Virginia Midland Railway, the Southern Railway's predecessor railroad. The two railroad lines once crossed at-grade until the traffic of both railroads became too much to handle. The solution the two companies agreed upon remains in operation today. It features a track that parted from the north side of the Washington Southern tracks at Seminary Stop, just a half-mile west of AF Tower. Here, a long arcing track brought the Washington Southern tracks onto a bridge above the tracks of the Southern Railway.

GS Block, later known as CW Tower, stood on the north side of Pohick Creek.[8]

There, the Washington Southern continued southwest, and the Southern Railway continued northwest.

As technology got better over time, railroad operators presided over tracks from long distances. Taking the place of the interlocking towers was a form of centralized traffic control from the RF&P Railroad headquarters in Richmond. Under the new centralized system, a single train dispatcher in Richmond now had complete control of the switches and signals over the entire length of the track. Control boards provided their operators a scale model picture of the track they managed and what switch points they controlled. This was a large console with a series of lines depicting tracks, switches and other miscellaneous track structures for the entire length of the railroad line. Electronic information concerning the progress of a train transmits to the control office instantly as a train passes through a section of track. At each track switch depicted on the console, there was a small light blub and a small lever. When the light bulb turned off, that meant a train was occupying that block and if the train needed to transfer to another track, the operator sitting miles away could simply turn the lever or push a button. Instantly a signal sent to the relay box out on the track in turn operated a motor for the switch that put the train onto another track.

The new system saved trains an average of forty seconds of time for every mile on its route. Importantly, it permitted trains to make up time without delaying other trains by carefully scheduling the use of different tracks. Not only did the railroad's effectiveness improve, but a corresponding decline in expenses was also something the RF&P Railroad management found irresistible. No longer needing the manned signal towers with this amazing new technology, the railroad began to demolish these structures. By early 1971, the RF&P Railroad had become the nation's first railroad to have centralized electronic traffic control for every mile of track in its system.

Chapter Eight
THE LINE EARNS ITS SPURS

ഇ൫

"If you come to a fork in the road, take it."
– Yogi Berra

ഇ൫

You can still see traces of a little railroad in the woods near Lorton. A roadbed that once carried mighty locomotives now bears the pounding footsteps of joggers on the Cross County Trail. The Engineering Division of the District of Columbia Department of Corrections ran the railroad later called the Lorton and Occoquan Railroad. Its only function was transportation for the District of Columbia's prison in Virginia. In 1909, Washington was running out of parcels of open space. The District of Columbia government, under the encouragement of President Theodore Roosevelt, acquired

1,150 acres in Virginia to build a unique prison. It was "conceived to render to the lawbreaker committed to its keeping a different method of treatment and care, based on sane, practical ideals designed to teach the unfortunate assurance, self-respect, and a more correct version of that which means for the general betterment." In other words, this was not a prison, but a "reformatory" where a convict might learn a trade skill, be educated and pay for their food and boarding. The prisoners came to Lorton because they had displayed good behavior at their former prisons.[1]

The District of Columbia government acquired the land through condemnation proceedings in 1910 and opened for inmates in 1916. Prisoners built their own dormitory buildings instead of cells. They used bricks the prisoners manufactured themselves on-site at the brickyard. The complex quickly gained notoriety due to Washington's response to the women's suffrage movement. In 1917, city police arrested 150 women for "obstructing traffic" while picketing for women's voting rights at the White House in Washington and sentenced them to the Lorton Reformatory. The guards mistreated the women at the reformatory, and on November 14 of that year, known as the "Night of Terror," Superintendent W. H. Whittaker met a group of 33 returning prisoners with dozens of guards who beat the women. They released the women from prison when national media outlets began to report on the story of their treatment.[2]

When the reformatory started, there were few area roads nearby. A ferry service was the only means to transport all the reformatory's supplies and inmates. It was the idea of the first Superintendent, Mr. Whittaker, to build a railroad to connect the far-flung areas of the reformatory by using a railway. Teams of inmates would work on constructing the railroad that would stretch nearly five miles over extremely hilly terrain. The workers used hand tools like picks and shovels, and construction moved slowly. In 1916, Superintendent Whittaker reported, "Without this railroad it would be an almost endless job for us to haul all of our building materials to the new reformatory site with teams. I estimate that it would require from 18 months to two years to fully complete and have practical operation of this railroad."[3] Completing the railroad and a siding connecting to the RF&P Railroad main line near Pohick Creek was the highest priority.

Superintendent Whittaker's original idea had been to use the railroad to transport prisoners between different buildings inside the reformatory, but with the enormous amount of construction material needed to build the reformatory in the first place, any dreams of using rail exclusively for passengers

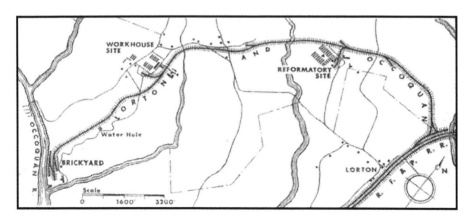

The Lorton and Occoquan Railroad stretched 4.5 miles in length upon its completion. Take note of the distances between the different reformatory areas on the map above, too far for a daily walk.[4]

ended. The superintendant ordered a powerful steam locomotive for freight operations. Engine #1 arrived by boat and immediately began pulling supplies and inmates to the many construction sites in the reformatory. In the year 1920, Superintendant Charles Foster introduced buses to take inmates from Washington to Lorton, ending the need for a ferry. However, the railroad was still important, and routine timetables were set up for transporting prisoners around the reformatory. The train itself was never a comfortable ride though, transporting up to sixty prisoners in just one or two boxcars bouncing along the hilly roadbed.[5]

Construction on the reformatory railroad reached the Richmond, Fredericksburg and Potomac Railroad near Pohick Creek in 1922. Bill Koch writes that, "the line still was not

Pictured here are the remains of a 40-foot wooden boxcar from the Lorton and Occoquan Railroad found in the woods by a Park Authority archaeologist in 2006 and restored.[6]

completely trustworthy and the Superintendent, upon his first inspection trip, had the locomotive stopped before crossing the wooden trestle over Giles Run. He waved the engine on, after he had safely walked to the other side of the trestle." The next decade would see the most traffic ever to cross the Lorton and Occoquan Railroad tracks. Bill Koch also writes in his Lorton history that Engine #1 proved to be the "best and sturdiest engine we ever had," according to Edison Lynn, the first engineer. "The first ten years we operated without air-brakes," he recalls, "and it was only pure luck that we never killed anybody going down those grades! I had to check the sand myself, and never let anyone else set my gauges. With the rough track and steep gauges you could never trust anyone else."

With the completion of the link to the RF&P Railroad, supplies that had been coming in by boat were now coming by rail from Washington. Food for the inmates and coal for the furnaces came in from the RF&P Railroad, as did fertilizer for the prison farm. Bricks and building materials went to the construction sites. On top of all that, the railroad was still busy shuttling inmates between the sites. Compounding the problem was the fact that the engine could only pull two loaded cars up the four percent grade from the RF&P Railroad and only one loaded car up the seven percent grade from the brickyard. Still, in 1960, the line managed to carry 85 million pounds of freight, and the engines ran up six thousand miles on the odometer. The entire railroad ran a distance of less than five miles. However, the extremely hilly terrain and a security check at the gate to meet the RF&P R.R.

Pictured here is the Barrel Arch Bridge at the Lorton Reformatory. Inmates at the reformatory constructed the bridge in 1946 from bricks they made themselves in the prison brickyard. The bridge crosses over the Lorton and Occoquan Railroad. The width of the tunnel is 23 feet. It is the only bridge of its kind in the state of Virginia.[7]

main line outside the reformatory would cause a trip to take more than thirty minutes.

The railroad was never an escape route to Lorton, and careful precautions made sure of that. They placed switches to derail the train at random places along the line, and the engineer had to search the train for any hidden inmates before the gates leading out from the reformatory opened. The brakes and track switches were always set so an engine could never accidentally roll down a hill.

The Lorton and Occoquan Railroad got rid of the steam engine in 1947 in favor of heavier diesel engines. They acquired two of these that had seen war service with the United States Army. When the railroad needed a boxcar or any other piece of equipment, a property agent would scout around the various governmental agencies looking for surplus equipment. When the railroads began scrapping their wooden boxcars in favor of metal boxcars, an agent from Lorton went to the Potomac Yard in Alexandria and procured two old wooden boxcars from the Baltimore and Ohio Railroad.

In the year 1970, overcrowding was a large issue at the reformatory. The government proposed that it could save money by purchasing ten Army hospital train cars and parking them on a spur to use as extra dormitories for the convicts instead of building new, permanent dormitories. When the prisoners promptly trashed the new cars and gave the security staff no end of trouble, they abandoned the proposal after only a few months. Ironically, that was not the end of the idea. The proposal of using extra trailers and train cars quickly came before county government officials, only this time the trailers would house extra classrooms for children at overcrowded schools around Fairfax County.

On an average day, the Lorton and Occoquan Railroad ran three round trip passenger trains between the workhouse and the brickyard in the morning, at lunch, and at the end of work in the afternoon. The number of runs along the rest of its length varied depending upon the amount of freight needing to move. It operated five days a week with emergency runs possible on Saturday. The line had been an integral part of the reformatory to transport its everyday supplies. The District of Columbia government shut down the rail line in the year 1977, and sold off most of the equipment within two or three years. The Lorton and Occoquan Railroad had run for 72 years. One engine is still in operation on an historic railroad in West Virginia. The reformatory closed in 2001 and operates now an arts center and water treatment facility. The roadbed today runs along a portion of the Gerald Connolly Cross County Trail, and the old rails now rest in the Lorton Museum.

The other major spur that connected to the Washington Southern Railway was the Fort Belvoir Military Railroad, so named after the estate established on the property in 1740. The elegant brick mansion called Belvoir belonged to William Fairfax. He was the area tax collector of his day and cousin to Lord Thomas Fairfax, from whom Fairfax County takes its name. The Belvoir mansion stood watch over the Potomac River for 43 years before a fire gutted it in 1783. During the War of 1812, American forces dug in on the slopes below the house during the four-day Naval Battle of the White House in 1814. What was left of the Belvoir mansion was destroyed by British cannon fire during the battle. The home foundations and adjacent family cemetery are on the National Register of Historic Places.[8]

In April of 1917, the United States declared war against Germany and entered the fighting in the First World War. At the same time, railroad executives from all across the nation met in Washington to discuss the best use of railroads in supplying the war effort. In an amazing show of patriotism, the railroads agreed to temporarily set aside their competitions with one another and form a nationalized railway system. To assist in the mobilization efforts of troops and supplies, President Woodrow Wilson created the United States Railroad Administration on December 26, 1917. This agency took over the operation of most of the country's railroads, including the Washington Southern Railway. Fortunately, the government handler for the Washington Southern was someone already very familiar with the railroad, William Duke, formerly the RF&P Railroad's General Superintendent. To alleviate stockholder's concerns, Director General of Railroads William McAdoo agreed to compensate the companies for their lost revenues while under federal control. He also agreed that the government would return all the equipment to the railroad in "as good repair as received" when hostilities ended overseas.

The U.S. Army purchased property on the Belvoir peninsula south of the town of Accotink in order to train and prepare engineers for combat in Europe. However, getting to the property was another matter entirely. In the closing months of 1917, Fairfax County was laboring through the harshest winter seen in decades. The county's muddy farm roads, especially the Accotink Turnpike and the King's Highway, were never intended to stand up to the snow or heavy hauling, and were practically impassable. It took six strong horses to pull an empty wagon down the King's Highway, and shipping was not an option either, as the Potomac River had frozen over. The construction of a dedicated military railroad was one of the first priorities.[9]

A five-mile-long railroad spur was to be constructed between the main line of the Washington Southern Railway at

Accotink Station and the site of Camp Andrew A. Humphreys (present-day Fort Belvoir), which was then under construction. On the morning of January 29, 1918, the Second Battalion of the 304th Engineers departed their headquarters at Camp Meade, Maryland, and arrived by train at Accotink Station three hours later, greeted by a whiteout blizzard. In true Army fashion, the men piled out of the train cars for their first ever backpack hike. Five miles of rugged forested country lay before them, and after trudging for hours through six inches of snow, they came to Camp Humphreys just as it began to darken. The barracks, when they reached them, were dirty and cold with just a folding canvas bunk to greet them.

The next day the raging blizzard continued as the men walked five miles with only a sandwich for their lunch to where their campsite was to be. There they worked in the snow all day, ate their cold lunch out in the open and brushed the snowflakes from their sandwiches as they ate. For a week thereafter, the men worked every day constructing their new camp. Mrs. George S. Kernan of the Mount Air plantation house played the kind host to the battalion on her land, and they named their encampment "Camp Merry Widow" in honor of her, while others, less grateful, give it the more obvious nickname of "Camp Mud."[10]

The Second Battalion began construction of the railroad from Accotink Station, while another group of engineers started to work from Camp Humphreys. Leaving the main railroad line, the proposed railroad right-of-way entered heavily wooded ground, crossed several valleys, plowed into a slight rise and

The photographs below depict the campsite of the Second Battalion of the 304th Engineers on the Mount Air property in 1918. At top is a general view of the campsite. In the middle, a soldier is improving the roadway through the campsite. At bottom is the officer's quarters.[11]

and passed their campsites. It skirted the village of Accotink and crossed several more valleys and streams until it arrived at Camp Humphreys.

The work required various jobs such as cutting timber, flattening hills, filling valleys and building four trestle bridges. The largest of these bridges was some six hundred feet long. The bridge would have a six-degree turn, a two percent grade, and require especially accurate workmanship. They measured and cut down timbers for the bridge from the surrounding forest. The men then hauled them from where they grew. Toward the end of the work, when extra speed was called for, they installed a series of electric lights around the bridge. Work continued both day and night. The battalion managed to complete this project and build passable roads through the area all in less than seventy-five days. The battalion left from Accotink and returned to their headquarters at Camp Meade,

This steam engine was kept busy on the light railway during the First World War.[12]

Maryland on April 14, 1918. These same engineers would be building bridges under German fire in France just a couple months later. The Allied victory would come in November of that year.

When the Fort Belvoir Military Railroad was finished, the power to pull the numerous boxcars, flatcars, coaches and Pullmans came from large steam engines supposedly used in building the Panama Canal. Two engines stayed busy during the First World War. When peace came, one became a stand-by engine. These locomotives ran from 1918 until about 1941 when diesels replaced them. Different engineering schools, including the Light Railway School, took advantage of the railroad as an instructional tool. There were units often seen learning the hands-on skills needed in building, maintaining and operating a railroad.

Camp Humphreys Storage Pile and Assembling Yard for the light railway.[13]

The Washington Southern Railway would remain under federal control for a total of 26 months. On February 29, 1920, by proclamation from the President of the United States, operational control over the railway was returned to the RF&P Railroad. They officially absorbed the Washington Southern Railway into their own system and the Washington Southern name relegated to the history books.

Over the years, Camp Andrew A. Humphreys continued to grow in size. Many of the area Quaker families lost their land to the fort's continued expansion and moved away. The name changed in 1935 to Fort Belvoir after President Franklin Roosevelt visited nearby Gunston Hall and learned of the historical associations with the Army property. The military railroad operated until 1997, a span of 79 years. The Base Realignment and Closure agreement, as well as the widening of Richmond Highway, meant the tracks and bridges were finally destroyed to bring the military into the twenty-first century.

Chapter Nine

THE MODERN ERA

൫ ൮

*"Both engines have failed and we will be
stuck here for some time. The good news is
that you decided to take the train and not fly."*
– Tim Davis

൫ ൮

During the Second World War, the RF&P Railroad sees traffic volumes staggeringly high along its line through Fairfax County. On April 22, 1943, over 33,000 passengers rode along the line, the most people ever recorded on a single day. The railroad would carry over eight million passengers in 1943, and nearly ten million military members in all rode the RF&P Railroad during the war. On average, a train ran every fourteen minutes during the war. Freight rail also played a large role in supplying the war effort, and it had lasting effects.

The post-war economic growth spread across all levels of society. It created a large and well-educated middle class that purchased goods from far-off companies shipping by train.[1]

During the war, the RF&P Railroad operated a standard double-track arrangement along its line. One track served southbound trains, and the other, northbound trains. In 1947, RF&P President Norman Call decided to build a third track between the interlock at South Franconia (near the old Ravenworth Stop) and the city of Alexandria to deal with the increased volume of freight traffic on the route. Having a third track allowed faster trains to bypass slower trains without having to delay on a siding for many minutes. Rebuilt at the same time, the Franconia Road overpass gets a longer and wider span to accommodate the third track.

The era of the steam locomotive ended years ago in 1949, but people who never saw one in action somehow still miss it. Something about the old steam trains captures the collective imagination as nothing else can. Young children and adults who know only the long grey asphalt of an interstate highway or an airport runway still desire to hear the cry of a steam whistle and see a train pull into a station in a cloud of smoke. Upon seeing such a train, people often wonder why a diesel engine replaced these iron horses.

There can be no question that the Great Depression was a bad time to invest hard-earned money into experimenting with trains, but railroad companies had few other options. Because of the struggling economy in the thirties, railroad profits were precariously low. Passenger travel on the RF&P Railroad hit record lows in 1933, followed by freight traffic in

The bell from a Southern Railway steam locomotive now hangs above Olivet Episcopal Church to ring in the faithful every Sunday.[2]

1934. If railroad companies wanted to survive, they had to decrease their expenses and improve efficiency. The use of diesel locomotives seemed to fit with both goals. In terms of expenses, steam engines required expensive maintenance and large trained crews to work them. They needed regular cleaning and wide-ranging repairs, which left that steam engine on the tracks for the railroad company to use on average only twenty days every month. Diesel locomotives required only a single person to operate, a lesser amount of maintenance and could run for three months before missing a day of work for repair.

In terms of efficiency, diesel locomotives could travel faster and had a longer lifetime than steam engines. Diesel engines were fuel-efficient and did not need their crews to take repeated stops for more coal and water to keep running. Getting technical for a moment, steam engines only used five percent of their potential energy for actually moving the wheels. On the other hand, a diesel engine could put 25 percent of its potential energy into moving the train. Traditionally, railroad executives thought that heavier trains were safer. However, because diesel engines were ten times lighter than a steam locomotive, the fuel efficiency drastically improved, as did safety records.[3]

Around most of the country, the switchover from steam to diesel was slow, but inexorable. Yet when the time came, the changeover was immediate on the Richmond, Fredericksburg and Potomac Railroad. In December of 1949, diesel engines replaced all the steam locomotives in a matter of days. The diesels had relegated steam engines to museums and sideshows, but nostalgia is strong. A bell liberated from a retiring Southern Railway steam locomotive hangs to this day above historic Olivet Episcopal Church at the intersection of Franconia Road and Beulah Street to ring in the faithful to service on Sundays.[4]

In 1952, Frank Parr built the massive Parr-Franconia Warehouse Complex located on Loisdale Road. Its flagship warehouse had the largest wooden roof truss system east of the Mississippi River at the time. When completed, the complex offered a staggering total of 1.5 million square feet of storage space. Upon reaching an agreement with the RF&P Railroad, they extended the old Ravensworth railroad siding into the complex. The warehouses are located on the western side of the main RF&P Railroad line. The spur formed the shape of a letter "C." For access, the spur branched off from the main line south of the warehouses where a counter-clockwise 270-degree turn brought trains across today's Metropolitan Center Drive and facing eastward so they could pull in alongside each of the warehouse storage units for easy loading and unloading.

The tale of the property's ownership is an interesting one. Frank D. Parr, a devout Methodist from San Francisco, had

This county aerial survey photograph looking to the southwest captured the Parr-Franconia Warehouse in 1953. Note the tracks of the railroad spur at the bottom of the photograph and running between the warehouses.[5]

built up a fortune in commercial real estate over his lifetime. In 1954, Parr was looking to sell his properties to the Methodist church. The legal advisor for the church at the time was Paul R. Russell who practiced law at Shearman, Sterling and Wright in New York City. Mr. Russell was a member of the struggling Park Avenue Methodist Church in New York, and arranged the sale of the warehouse here in Franconia to that church. The rental revenues over the years allowed the church to become solvent and embark on new community programs. When the federal government bought the property outright in 1966, Mr. Russell created a trust fund for the church.

The General Services Administration has been the major tenant at the Parr-Franconia Warehouse Complex since its inception. The RF&P Railroad gave the stop the name of Ravensworth, spelled with an "S" this time, unlike the original 1872 stop nearby and allowed local passenger traffic to board near the foot of Barry Road. The name Ravensworth pays homage to the original Fitzhugh family land grant that covered most of Springfield, including the land upon which the warehouse stands. The stop was a busy one for the local freight trains, handling hundreds of rail cars every month. After 48 years of service, the government removed the tracks in 2000 to make way for the Springfield Crossing apartment complex built on the north side of the property.

The post-war boom in passenger traffic was a short one. By 1950, only half as many people were riding trains than were before the Second World War. This is thanks in large part to the rise of the freedom and convenience of automobile travel and the establishment of the National Highway System. In Fairfax County, the biggest competitor to the RF&P Railroad was the Henry G. Shirley Highway. Built in sections between 1941 and 1952, Shirley Highway stretched for seventeen miles between Woodbridge in the south and the Fourteenth Street Bridge over the Potomac River in the north. It directly parallels the RF&P Railroad line for ten miles of its length. The state named the highway in honor of the commissioner of the Virginia Department of Highways, Henry Shirley. He had approved this project for construction only three weeks before his death in 1941.

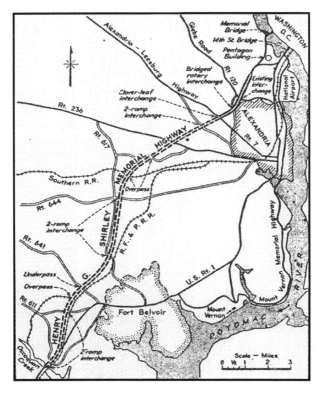

This map by state engineer A. H. Hill shows Shirley Highway completed only to Route 7 in 1946. The extension south to the Occoquan River had yet to be constructed.[6]

By 1953, this focus on developing roads and highways built up demand in a new industry, long-haul truckers. It was becoming cheaper and faster for goods to move by truck rather than by a train car. This disparity caused the RF&P Railroad to lose business from the United States Post Office Department to trucks and planes. Mail delivery by train had once been the only reliable method for news and information outside of one's own village. At its peak, the revenues from mail delivery doubled the combined revenue brought in from passenger train service.

RF&P Railroad President Norman Call had observed a shift away from local passenger service to more freight service on his line. For the shareholders of his company, it paid to prioritize freight traffic, because passenger trains predictably impede freight trains trying to run the same route faster and hurting the company's potential profits. To tighten the budget and speed up service, Norman Call decided to close the underused passenger stop at Franconia Station, which had rendered eighty-two years of service to the neighborhood. In Fairfax County, the axe spared only the major stations at Accotink and Lorton for the time being.

Accotink Station was renamed Newington Station the following year. The name change better reflected the neighborhood that grew up around the station in the past eighty years, becoming its own distinct community from its neighbors. The name Newington comes from Richard Nevitt, who was the owner of the Newington house in 1872 when the railroad came through his property, until it burned down in April of 1875. Oral history stated that it was the oldest house standing in Fairfax County at the time. Today you can visit the roadside marker at the entrance to Levelle W. Dupell Park on Newington Road. The private family cemetery is located nearby.

Even considering the decline in passenger service, nostalgia for an old-fashioned train ride was strong. For years, the RF&P Railroad ran a wildly popular caboose special for a number of groups, including military veterans, families, and the National Railway Historical Society. On one occasion in 1958, over seven hundred people purchased tickets for a sightseeing ride from Alexandria's Union Station to Richmond. An old steam engine led the train, with the passengers enjoying the sights in eight coach cars and fifteen cabooses. The passengers rode halfway in a coach car and halfway in a caboose. The tour included rides around the Richmond railroad facilities and photo opportunities with old locomotives. The participating families declared the event a rousing success. Repeats of the caboose special in following years included stops for military families at Fort Belvoir.

Early in his career, Academy Award winning director Arthur Cohn immortalized Franconia's iron roads on the silver screen. In 1959, filming for his documentary film "Sidetracked" brought the noted producer to Newington. The film's storyline follows an investigation into a chemical plant disaster and missing railroad cars that could explode at any moment. The filming of the climatic chase scene occurred along the tracks near Lorton. The film crew rode back and forth several times between the stations at Woodbridge and Newington to get the perfect take, while the

RF&P Railroad train dispatcher worked to keep the regularly scheduled trains from disrupting the filming process. Most of the actors in the film were regular employees of the railroad, who ran the empty train back and forth for the cameras. Director Cohn preferred a more realistic touch to his films, and chose to use railroad workers who were accustomed to doing the job as a part of their everyday life instead of actors.

Because of the country's dependence on cars and the growing attractiveness of airline travel, the declining use of passenger trains continued through the sixties. Private railroads became a popular punching bag for lawmakers and construction companies who wanted public funding for road building projects. The railroad companies themselves did not want government involvement in their businesses, and did little to counter this growing anti-railroad perception. The tipping point came when previously dominant railroad companies started filing for bankruptcy, including the Pullman Company and the Penn Central Railroad (a successor of the Pennsylvania Railroad who originally built the Alexandria and Fredericksburg line). Suddenly, stunned lawmakers watched commerce screech to a halt in some areas, as there were no solvent companies left to operate the trains. Lawmakers deemed some railroads as too important to fail and set public-private partnerships in motion to save them.

To counter the downward trend in passenger rail service, the United States Congress passed the Rail Service Passenger Act of 1970. This legislation established the National Railroad Passenger Corporation. The mission Congress gave them was to take over the passenger routes operated by private railroad companies. Congress gave the railroad companies an ultimatum: to either continue operating current passenger rail services in perpetuity or turn over those services to the National Railroad Passenger Corporation, who would then operate the route.

The RF&P Railroad signed on, as did other passenger railroads around the country. The National Railroad Passenger Corporation replaced all of the RF&P passenger trains with its novel new service called Amtrak. Amtrak began service on May 1, 1971 serving 43 states with a total of 21 routes. The routes at the beginning were just routes the local trains were already running. Amtrak often used the same

Viewed from the King Street Metro platform, Amtrak Engine No. 199 pulls away from Alexandria's Union Station with the George Washington Masonic Memorial towering in the background.[7]

train cars purchased straight from the railroads they took over, still painted with the old color schemes of their previous owners. Amtrak also had priority on the same tracks run by the freight railroads, but with overcrowded routes, trains ended up delayed for everyone, passenger or freight. In the end, many freight companies found it easier to send their trains along other routes to avoid the Alexandria area, which hurt the RF&P Railroad.

Unfortunately, Amtrak initially chose to bypass Fairfax County for stops in more populated areas. The RF&P Railroad then shuttered its local passenger stations along the line, including Newington and Lorton Stations. It is interesting to note that service to both stations fell short of the century mark by just a single year, having been in existence for ninety-nine years. Decades later, Amtrak did temporarily place a stop on its Northeast Regional Service at the Franconia-Springfield Station between 1997 and 2010, to mixed results. Amtrak receives taxpayer funding in exchange for providing passenger rail service, but has never turned a profit due to competition from planes and cars.[8]

Also in 1971, a wildly successful passenger route started called the Auto Train. The Auto Train runs for 855 miles between Lorton Station and the town of Sanford, Florida, just minutes outside of Orlando. Often billed as the longest passenger train in the world, it is a daily train service run for passengers and their vehicles. The passengers can ride in coaches or sleeper cars while their vehicles (be it car, van or motorcycle) ride on specially designed auto racks. Connected together, the train can include fifty railcars and stretch for

over 4,000 feet, nearly a mile in length. It is the only one of
its kind operated in the United States. It allows passengers to
avoid the traffic on Interstate 95 or the crowded airport
terminals, while still bringing their own car with them.
Passengers leave the station at 4:00 p.m. one day and arrive
the next morning at 9:00 a.m. at their destination. Service
temporarily halted in the year 1981 when the Auto Train
Corporation ran into financial hardship and declared
bankruptcy. That was due to bad routes created in western
states, not the Lorton to Sanford route. Amtrak then took
over the service in 1983. The Auto Train often wins awards
for its high quality equipment and great customer service. It
also pulls in about fifty million dollars in revenues every year,
making it Amtrak's best performing train and the official train
of Walt Disney World Resorts.[9]

Shown on a summer morning in 1999, the Lorton Auto Train terminal
prepares to receive passengers and cars for its daily run to Florida.
Amtrak built a larger facility on the same site in the year 2000.[10]

A day on the Auto Train is a busy one for the railroad workers. Station gates open at 11:30 a.m. for passengers to drive their car to a staging area. There, a magnet with a unique car number is placed on the driver's door and the car is scanned for preexisting damages, in case someone files a claim later. The passengers leave their car and go to the station to await boarding. Workers arrange the vehicles by size into the best loading order and then put them on the auto racks. The workers then connect all the passenger cars and auto racks together into one long train, and passengers come aboard an hour before it departs at 4:00 p.m. At midnight, train crews quickly stop in Florence, South Carolina to refuel the engines and change crews. The train finally arrives at its destination at 9:00 a.m. where workers separate the train cars and the vehicles are unloaded from the auto racks, a process that can take two hours with a full train.[11]

For many years, the area now known as Kingstowne was nothing but unsightly sand and gravel pits as far as the eye could see. Yet, in 1972, a private developer called the Nilsen Group from New Hope, Pennsylvania came forward with a grand vision for the area, a plan to make the area useful and beautiful again. The planned community called "New Franconia" would sit on about 2,000 acres of land stretching between Beulah Street and Telegraph Road. It would house more than 40,000 people.[12]

The most distinctive feature of the planned community would be the monorail. It would offer free rides to everyone on ten-minute intervals around the clock using quiet electric-powered trains. To guarantee easy access, all stations would be no more than a one-minute ride apart. This monorail would have at least nine stations to connect all the sections of the planned town together and even connect residents with the RF&P Railroad line and the new Washington Metro subway line planned for Franconia Station.[13]

In short, the town would be so attractive to residents that they would choose to take the rail system and leave their cars at home. Half of all people in the planned community would live less than five hundred feet away from a monorail station. In some of the early drawings from the Nilsen Group, the monorail partially follows the course of what is today the Kingstowne Village Parkway between South Van Dorn Street and Beulah Street.[14]

Unfortunately, the Fairfax County Board of Supervisors did not approve the zoning changes needed in order to build the community, and the Nilsen Group abandoned the project at the close of 1973. However, Lee District Supervisor Joseph Alexander was still interested in bringing community development to the area rather than more heavy industry. It would take another decade for developer Warren Halle to form the Kingstowne Residential Owners Corporation out of the ashes of the New Franconia plan. Groundbreaking finally occurred in 1986, and the Kingstowne community celebrates its thirtieth anniversary this year... without a monorail.[15]

In 1973, the Franconia neighborhood gets a pipeline. Originally constructed by affiliates of Shell, Texaco, Chevron and Exxon, the Plantation Pipeline came about during the Second World War. That pipeline carried fuel from Baton Rouge, Louisiana to Greensboro, North Carolina. Extended into Virginia as far as Newington in 1964, it built another extension in 1973 from Newington to Washington National Airport following the right-of-way of the RF&P Railroad through the Franconia neighborhood. This pipeline currently supplies jet fuel for aircraft at the airport.

In 1974, the RF&P Railroad removed the third rail line built back in 1947 from Franconia to Alexandria, returning to double track service. This contributed to a substantial rail traffic decline. However, the RF&P Railroad found success over the decades in keeping local freight alive by operating a number of short spurs for warehouses along its line. Former passenger stops such as Seminary, Bush Hill, Lunt, Franconia and Newington all got warehouse spurs. For example, the Fleet Industrial Park came to Franconia in 1977 and had a railroad spur extended from the RF&P Railroad main line near Fleet Drive into its warehouses. One of the biggest beneficiaries was the tenant Xerox. The spur serviced the complex for 32 years before removal in 2009.

If there is just one train that people always recall with great fondness, it is the "Great White Juice Train." Starting in the year 1970, the Tropicana Products Company began shipping one million gallons of orange juice from Florida to New Jersey in insulated and refrigerated boxcars each week. The train consisted of 150 distinctive white cars emblazoned with the company logo on the side. Tropicana reported saving close to forty million dollars just in fuel expenses during the first decade that the train ran. The Great White Juice Train continues to receive awards for efficiency, and is a good example of how freight rail still competes favorably against trucks, ships and other means of transportation.

The Fruit Growers Express Company manufactured the Tropicana cars at its Alexandria facility, with the cars each weighing in at 100 tons. Also known as FGE, they manufactured refrigerated cars for fruits and vegetables, but also repaired, designed and built new rail cars to transport just about any perishable product. The facility was located at Seminary Station, west of the Telegraph Road overpass. Today, South Quaker Lane borders the property on the west and Roth Street on the east. FGE manufactured railroad cars for many different railroads at that facility between 1926 and 1971, and its company roots go back another 20 years at Potomac Yard. They were the largest industrial employer in the City of Alexandria with over 500 employees on site.

Alexandria's Fruit Growers Express Company in 1971.[16]

There was an interesting story to come from RF&P Railroad worker John Frye, who often spent time working the tracks in the Franconia area. He recalls the telephone-like cables that carried signals all along the railroad to switch trains from track to track. Normally, the system worked reliably, but starting fluctuating unpredictably one month. After days of walking along the tracks looking for the trouble, Frye finally saw a young kid with a rifle attempting to shoot birds off the signal wires. Most of the shots had apparently missed the birds, but tore up the signal wires instead, leaving dozens of holes to be repaired![17]

In 1978, the RF&P Railroad proposed installing a controversial 240-foot-tall microwave communications tower abutting the track at the west end of Howells Road off Valley View Drive as part of the company's $2 million plan to upgrade its communications system linking Richmond to Northern Virginia. The RF&P Railroad wanted to do away with the outdated pole and cable signal system. Residents who lived around the tower site voiced strong concerns over the radiation levels emitted by the tower and the effect it would have on personal health. There was also a concern that the unsightly structure would lower property values in the surrounding residential neighborhoods.[18]

The RF&P Railroad defended itself by saying that the radiation emitted by the tower would be lower than "the strictest world standards." Railroad representatives said the tower could withstand 150-mile-per-hour winds and looked nicer than the pole and cable system currently in place. Public hearings about the tower occurred at Saint Lawrence Catholic

Former Fairfax County Supervisor Joseph Alexander, whose district the radio tower proposal affected, is shown here leading a community talk at the Franconia Museum in 2015.[19]

Church on Franconia Road, the closest building to the tower site able to accommodate the large crowds. In the end, Lee District Supervisor Joseph Alexander, along with the rest of the Fairfax County Board of Supervisors, agreed to a compromise with the railroad to keep the tower.[20]

Here in Virginia, the railroad companies themselves owned the railroad tracks and the right-of-way. Land grants by the federal government to the railroads from the very beginning allowed this to happen. Furthermore, freight railroad companies today are privately owned and operated, with no government subsidies. While railroads own some of the thousands of freight cars they use, the shipping companies actually own most of them. Part of the reason for the decline in freight rail traffic in the middle of the twentieth century was regulation by the federal government. They set the fees that railroads could charge, among many other regulations. By 1970, the railroads were nearly bankrupt. Congress could either deregulate the railroads or nationalize them. Lawmakers opted for the former.

The United States Congress approved two important pieces of legislation toward achieving this goal. They were the Railroad Revitalization and Regulatory Reform Act (or 4R Act) of 1976 and the Staggers Rail Act of 1980. Both acts gave private railroads the freedom to determine their own freight routes, set prices for moving freight and streamline procedures to prevent abuses. They also helped Amtrak to increase the number of passenger routes it provided. Since the acts passed, private railroads have become more competitive and have increased their revenues and volume of freight traffic significantly.

How the RF&P Railroad came under the ownership of the CSX Corporation is simply the result of mergers among the six companies that owned the RF&P Railroad under the 1901 formation of the Richmond-Washington Company. CSX Corporation formed in 1987 through a merger of Chessie System and Seaboard System. Chessie and Seaboard came about through the mergers of four of the RF&P Railroad's six original owners, the Baltimore and Ohio, the Chesapeake and Ohio, the Atlantic Coast Line and the Seaboard Air Line. Therefore, CSX had two-thirds ownership of the RF&P Railroad. By 1989, the other two of the six original owners, the Norfolk Southern Railway and Conrail (successor to the Pennsylvania Railroad) eventually sold their ownership in the RF&P Railroad to CSX. In 1991, the last stakeholder, the government of Virginia, sold its remaining shares in the RF&P Railroad. It merged into the CSX system and officially ceased to operate as an independent entity after 157 years of service.[21]

Even before the RF&P Railroad had closed Newington Station, the last passenger rail station in the Franconia area in 1971, plans were already moving forward on a new project to bring commuter rail service back to the Franconia area in the form of the Washington Metro subway system. Construction began in the District of Columbia in 1969, but expansion along the existing RF&P Railroad right-of-way into Fairfax County would not occur for twenty more years. Metro officials had acquired land for the Van Dorn Street Station as early as 1977, and plans for expanding to Springfield were on paper by 1986, yet funding delays hampered progress. It would not be until June 15, 1991, that Metro finally extended service to the Van Dorn Street Station.

The choice of the Van Dorn name is an interesting one. The roadway formerly known as the Old Lincolnia Road or Triplett Lane was a part of Fairfax County until 1952. Upon annexation by the City of Alexandria, a law on the books required all new north-south streets in the city to have names honoring Confederate military officers. In 1953, the road was renamed Van Dorn Street to honor Major General Earl Van Dorn, shown here.[22]

Born in 1820 in Mississippi, Van Dorn would embark on a career as an Army officer fighting with distinction in the Mexican War and the tribal wars. During the American Civil War, he served as a major general in the Confederate Army of Tennessee. Called "the terror of ugly husbands," his womanizing ways repeatedly landed him into trouble. In May of 1863, Doctor James Peters claimed Van Dorn had an affair with his wife while using his home as a headquarters building. Peters snuck into the office with Van Dorn and shot him in the back, killing him instantly. He would be the only general to die of "private problems" during the war.

Van Dorn Street Station remained the southwestern terminus of the Blue Line for six years. In 1997, Metro extended the tracks out to Franconia-Springfield Station. It is located just to the south of Springfield Mall on the site of the former Windsor Stop on the Alexandria and Fredericksburg Railway. However, early plans could have had the Metro system looking very different in the Franconia neighborhood.

In early drafts brought by the Washington Metropolitan Area Transit Authority, especially in the 1969 plan, the Blue Line trains would continue west out of Van Dorn Street Station and split in two. One line would directly follow the RF&P Railroad right-of-way to serve a terminus at "Franconia Metro Station." Metro officials considered building this station just north of Franconia Road on the property where the old Franconia railroad station was located for many years. The plan also allowed for an extension south to Fort Belvoir, Woodbridge or points beyond.

In addition, the Blue Line trains would continue west out of Van Dorn Street Station and run to a second terminus. Travelling between the Southern Railway tracks to the north and the Capital Beltway to the south, the Blue Line would reach its other terminus at the "Backlick Road Metro Station" where today the historic Springfield Station stands to serve the Virginia Railway Express line to Manassas. The plan also allowed for a Blue Line extension west through Springfield, Burke and points beyond.[23]

Known as the "J" route, the proposed extension kept appearing for a few years in the published maps. Local resistance to a Metro station at the former Franconia Station site ultimately killed the proposed route. Residents of the neighborhood, lead by future Land Use Committee chairman Liles Creighton, were wary of putting a high-density project like a subway station adjacent to the many low-density bedroom communities that had developed in the area. A second look at the plan showed the wisdom in placing the station in a higher-density area like the Springfield Mall, which had just opened for business to rousing crowds and visits from the British royal family. With Metro officials already considering the running of two separate branch lines as too costly, the two planned stations at Franconia and Backlick Road combined into the one Franconia-Springfield Station that exists today.

However, the limited service run by Amtrak and Metro in the early nineties was not frequent enough to meet the needs of the increasing number of commuters in the suburbs further away from the city of Alexandria. Despite pushback from

CSX Transportation to running more passenger service along its crowded freight line, enough local governments banded together to create the Virginia Railway Express. Service began in June of 1992 using the CSX-owned tracks in place between Washington's Union Station and Fredericksburg, Virginia. Trains began stopping at a rebuilt Lorton Station in 1994, and a temporary Franconia-Springfield Station in 1995 to serve the Fredericksburg Line of the Virginia Railway Express. Serving about five million commuter trips annually, the success of the Virginia Railway Express proved the potential that still exists in passenger rail service. Private railroads had always been skeptical and cautious of working with federal and state governments, and this partnership was truly a historic event.[24]

The next decade saw a rail resurgence based off this success. In 1997, the completion of Metrorail to Franconia-Springfield Station meant the sprawling Joe Alexander Transportation Center south of the Springfield Mall complex was complete. Entering into the twenty-first century, the Virginia Railway Express commuter trains added more runs each year as passenger volume grew.

CSX Transportation also chose to expand its freight services and rebuilt the third rail on its line between South Franconia and Alexandria. Adding back the third track eased overcrowding and improved the reliability of the train schedules. Having this third track also allowed CSX to compensate for bottlenecks, particularly during the rush hour periods in the morning and evening when they had to accommodate the larger number of Amtrak, commuter and

The Joe Alexander Transportation Center now stands near the site of Windsor Stop.[25]

freight trains. In particular, it mitigated the congestion caused by the still ever-present Franconia Grade by allowing the faster Amtrak and commuter trains to overtake the slower freight trains on the hill.[26]

Increasingly, the state government in Richmond underwent a subtle shift in their policy toward railroads. Some lawmakers wanted to put passenger railroad service on the same "guaranteed" level with providing mail delivery and public road access. They wanted to protect the railroad lines that had managed to survive for future generations to use. It could have been easy to sell off the land and tear up the railroad tracks to make way for more residential and commercial development, a fate that had already occurred to nearby Potomac Yard in Alexandria and to other railroads in western Fairfax County.[27]

In a historic effort lead by Governor Mark Warner in 2005, the General Assembly created the Virginia Rail Enhancement Fund as a way to bypass the state constitutional ban on public financing of railroads. Railroads can now gain public financing by simply proving to the state government that the construction project would bring more public benefit than the dollar investment spent in state funds. A state tax on automobile rentals sustains the fund that works to save railroad infrastructure for the future.[28]

The railroad line that started with the Alexandria and Fredericksburg Railway 144 years ago still has it all. For those who want to pause and look out over the Franconia Road overpass at the snaking iron line dividing our communities today, dividing Franconia and Springfield, dividing the high schools of Thomas A. Edison and Robert E. Lee, they can see history continuing to rumble by. On average, Amtrak and CSX each run over twenty trains a day and the Virginia Railway Express commuter train routes add another eight daily trains. It shows those rails are still a happening place, with fifty trains running every weekday.

What the future may hold is an open question. Advocates for commuter rail service want to extend tracks to Fort Belvoir and lead the revitalization of Richmond Highway. With the success of high-speed rail overseas, the prospect of boarding a train in Washington and arriving in another city faster than airplane travel excites the imagination. Advocates of freight rail service see trains as an environmentally friendlier option than the many trucks clogging up the local highways. Advances in speed, safety, automation and clean energy all promise to revolutionize the rail industry over the coming decades. To quote Cory Booker, "For an economy built to last, we must invest in what will fuel us for generations to come. This is our history. Our American ancestors prioritized growth and investment in our nation's infrastructure."[29]

Chapter Ten

RAILFAN PHOTO GALLERY

ဢဢ

"Old railfans never die, they just lose track."
- Unknown

ဢဢ

The following pages exemplify the efforts of the Richmond, Fredericksburg and Potomac Railroad Historical Society, Inc. based in Fredericksburg. Join them today at www.rfandp.org. Their members seek to promote and preserve the history of the RF&P Railroad through education, historical and technical research, preservation and modeling. One of the best local photographers was Bruce Fales of Silver Spring, Maryland, who passed on in 1993. He had a unique way of capturing action shots that brought trains to life, even in an old gray photograph. This is their story of Franconia told in pictures:

Above: RF&P Railroad Engine No. 301, with Train No. 15, a local between Washington and Richmond, climbs the Franconia grade southbound arriving at Franconia Station in 1939. **Below:** RF&P Railroad Engine No. 325 arrives northbound into Franconia Station. Both photographs come from the Bruce Fales Collection courtesy of the RF&PRRHS.

Above: RF&P Railroad Engine No. 307 pulls into Franconia Station northbound for Potomac Yard. **Below:** RF&P Railroad Engine No. 502 crests the top of Franconia Hill southbound at milepost 99.0, located underneath the Old Franconia Road overpass. Both photographs come from the Bruce Fales Collection courtesy of the RF&PRRHS.

Above: RF&P Railroad Engine No. 502 with an auxiliary tender passes southbound with Franconia Station shown in the background. Photograph taken from the Franconia Road overpass. **Below:** RF&P Railroad Engine No. 326 pulls northbound into Franconia Station. Both photographs come from the Bruce Fales Collection courtesy of the RF&PRRHS.

Above: RF&P Railroad Engine No. 303 arrives southbound at Franconia Station, with passengers shown waiting at right. **Below:** RF&P Railroad Engine No. 579 passes Franconia Station northbound in 1946 with 62 empty Fruit Growers Express empty refrigerator cars. Both photographs come from the Bruce Fales Collection courtesy of the RF&PRRHS.

Above: An RF&P Railroad Engine passes Franconia Station with freight cars northbound for Potomac Yard. **Below:** RF&P Railroad Engine No. 573 arrives southbound at the Lunt Flag Stop near today's South Van Dorn Street, where a passenger awaits a train. Both photographs come from the Bruce Fales Collection courtesy of the RF&PRRHS.

Above: RF&P Railroad Engine No. 577 nears the top of the Franconia grade with 72 cars southbound in 1946. Note the Franconia schoolhouse shown on the hill to the left. **Below:** RF&P Railroad Engine No. 552 travels southbound from Franconia Station. Both photographs come from the Bruce Fales Collection courtesy of the RF&PRRHS.

Above: RF&P Railroad Engine No. 601, known as the Governor Patrick Henry, travels southbound past the Ravensworth Flag Stop in the year 1943. Photograph by Homer Hill courtesy of the RF&PRRHS. **Below:** Accotink Station became a centerpiece in its community, but as the picture shows, it took time for the community to grow up around it! Photograph courtesy of the Franconia Museum.

Workers clear the railroad path in a process called grading. Photographs come courtesy of the Franconia Museum.

Engineers work to construct bridges across the hilly terrain. Photographs come courtesy of the Franconia Museum.

Engineers work to construct bridges across the hilly terrain. Photographs come courtesy of the Franconia Museum.

Laborers work to lay many miles of track for the railroad. Photographs come courtesy of the Franconia Museum.

Chapter Eleven

SOURCE REFERENCES

ঔ৩ ৎ৪

*"So if you read this far, you were not wasting your
time. Other people have things to teach you."*
– Kevin Thompson

ঔ৩ ৎ৪

Covers and Introductions

Cover: Hopkins, Griffith Morgan, Jr. Atlas of fifteen miles around Washington, including the
county of Montgomery, Maryland. Philadelphia: G.M. Hopkins, 1878. Map. Retrieved
from the Library of Congress, https://www.loc.gov/item/87675339. Accessed January 8,
2016. Photograph is in the public domain and comes from the Library of Congress
Geography and Map Division, Washington, D.C.

Cover: Herman, Herman, Russell, Andrew J, photographer. "Engine 'Gen. Haupt,' Alexandria,
1863." 1863. Image. https://www.loc.gov/item/2004680117. Accessed November 25,
2015. Photograph is in the public domain and comes from the Library of Congress Prints
and Photographs Division, Washington, D.C.

Cover: Photograph of the interlock tower at Pohick Creek used with permission from the
archive files of the Franconia Museum, 6121 Franconia Road, Alexandria, Virginia.
Original photographer unknown.

Cover: Lee, Nathaniel. "VRE at Franconia" 2015. JPEG file. Photograph taken by the author.

Cover: Photograph of the Franconia train station used with the permission of Franconia Museum, Inc., 6121 Franconia Road, Alexandria, Virginia 22310.

Contents: Lavy, John S. "Railroad Track Border." October 10, 2010. Accessed September 30, 2015. http://www.dreamstime.com/royalty-free-stock-images-railroad-track-border-image27806629. Border image reproduced with permission from John Lavy.

Page i: Griffin Jr., William E. "Richmond, Fredericksburg & Potomac Railroad: Capital Cities Route." 1st ed. Forest, Virginia: TLC Publishing, 1994. 21. Timeline of presidents for the Richmond, Fredericksburg and Potomac Railroad Company.

Page i: Klebe, Alexandra and Vicki Brightbill. "All Aboard the Pennsy." Pennsylvania Center for the Book. April 16, 2009. Accessed September 27, 2015. http://pabook.libraries.psu.edu/palitmap/PARR.html. Information on the Presidents of the Pennsylvania Railroad.

Page ii: Lee, Nathaniel. "Railroad Stations map." 2015. PNG file. Drawn using the open data service from Fairfax County's Geographic Information System and Mapping Service Branch, Fairfax, Virginia. Accessed September 23, 2015. http://www.fairfaxcounty.gov/maps.

Author page: Lee, Nathaniel. "Nathaniel sketching." 2015. JPEG file. Photograph taken by the author.

Chapter 1: The Southern Gateway

1: Norton, Mary Beth. "A People and a Nation: A History to 1877." New York, New York: Houghton Mifflin Company, 2007. Information regarding the South's view of carpetbaggers.

2: "A History of Roads in Virginia." Richmond, Virginia: Virginia Department of Transportation. 2006. Information on transportation in antebellum Virginia.

3: Magnus, Charles. "Birds Eye View of Alexandria, Va." The Library of Congress. 1864. Accessed November 20, 2015. http://www.loc.gov/resource/g3884a.pm009504. Artwork is in the public domain and comes from the Library of Congress Geography and Map Division, Washington, D.C.

4: Turner, Charles W. "Railroad Service to Virginia farmers, 1828-1860." Agricultural History. Volume 22, Number 4 (October 1948). Information on transportation in antebellum Virginia.

5: Puffert, Douglas J. "The Standardization of Track Gauge on North American Railways, 1830-1890." The Journal of Economic History. Volume 60, Number 4 (December 2000). Information regarding different track gauges in Virginia.

6: Netherton, Nan, Donald Sweig, Janice Artemel, Patricia Hickin and Patrick Reed. "Fairfax County, Virginia: A History." Fairfax, Virginia: Fairfax County Board of Supervisors. 1978. Information on railroad development in Fairfax County.

7: Forbes, Edwin. "Rebuilding the RR bridge over the Rappahannock River." The Library of Congress. May 6 1862. 1 drawing. Accessed September 27, 2015. http://lccn.loc.gov/2004661570. Artwork is in the public domain and comes from the Library of Congress Prints and Photographs Division, Washington, D.C.

8: Churella, Albert J. "Connections." In The Pennsylvania Railroad, Volume 1: Building an Empire, 1846-1917, 418-420. 1st ed. Vol. 1. Philadelphia, Pennsylvania: University of Pennsylvania Press, 2012. Information on Pennsylvania Railroad executives' states of mind during expansion years.

9: Ward, James A. "J. Edgar Thomson: Master of the Pennsylvania." Santa Barbara, California: Praeger Publishing. 1980.

10: Scharf, Thomas J. and Thompson Westcott. History of Philadelphia, 1609-1884. Philadelphia, Pennsylvania: Louis H. Everts and Company, 1884. Sketch of Edgar Thomson is in the public domain and comes courtesy of the Pennsylvania Historical and Museum Commission Bureau for Historic Preservation, Commonwealth Keystone Building, Second Floor, 400 North Street, Harrisburg, Pennsylvania 17120-0093.

11: Ward, James A. "Power and Accountability on the Pennsylvania Railroad, 1846-1878." *The Business History Review* 49 (1). Cambridge, Massachusetts: Cambridge University Press. 37-59. http://www.jstor.org/stable/3112961. Regarding financials of the railroad.

12: Nace, Ted. "Gangs of America: The Rise of Corporate Power and the Disabling of Democracy." New York, New York: Berrett-Koehler Publishers. 2005. Information on railroad holding companies.

Chapter 2: The Long Way Around

1: Berg, Scott W. "Grand Avenues: The Story of the French Visionary Who Designed Washington, D.C." New York, New York: Pantheon Books. Information on how the railroads destroyed the design of DC.

2: Russell, Andrew J. "Potomac Creek Bridge, Aquia Creek & Fredericksburg Railroad, April 18, 1863." The Library of Congress. April 18, 1863. 1 photograph. Accessed November 20, 2015. http://hdl.loc.gov/loc.pnp/ppmsca.07299. Photograph is in the public domain and comes from the Library of Congress Prints and Photographs Division, Washington, D.C.

3: McGehee, C. Coleman, "I've been working on the railroad: the saga of the Richmond, Fredericksburg and Potomac Railroad Company." 1992. Master's Theses. Paper 752. http://scholarship.richmond.edu/masters-theses.

4: Vaisz, W and Virginia Board of Public Works. "Map of the proposed line of Rail Road connection between tide water Virginia and the Ohio River at Guyandotte, Parkersburg and Wheeling / made by W. Vaisz, topographical engineer for the Board of Public Works of Virginia." The Library of Congress. Map. Philadelphia. 1852. Accessed July 15, 2015. http://hdl.loc.gov/loc.gmd/g3881p.rr000810. Artwork is in the public domain and comes from the Library of Congress Geography and Map Division, Washington, D.C.

5: Johnston Jr., Angus James. "Virginia Railroads in the Civil War." Chapel Hill, North Carolina: University of North Carolina Press, 1961.

6: Pierpont, Francis H. "The Restored Government of Virginia – History of the New State of Things." *The New York Times*, June 26, 1864. Accessed December 14, 2016. http://www.nytimes.com/1864/06/26/news/virginia-the-restored-government-of-virginia-history-of-the-new-state-of-things.html.

7: Boyd Sipe, M.A. and Kimberly Snyder, M.A. "Documentary Study and Archaeological Resource Assessment for the James Bland Homes, City of Alexandria, Virginia." Gainesville, Virginia: Thunderbird Archaeology. 2010.

8: Macoll, John D. and George J. Stansfield. "Alexandria: A Towne in Transition, 1800-1900." Washington, District of Columbia: Moore and Moore, Inc. 1977.

9: Lee, Nathaniel. "Bank of Potomac Building." 2009. JPEG file. Photograph taken by the author.

10: "City Council Official Proceedings." Alexandria Gazette, June 27, 1866.

11: Kollner, Augustus. "Steamboat Wharf, Washington, D.C." The Library of Congress. 1839. 1 drawing. Accessed January 27, 2015. http://lccn.loc.gov/2004661949. Artwork is in the public domain and comes from the Library of Congress Prints and Photographs Division, Washington, D.C.

12: "Local News." Alexandria Gazette, December 15, 1870.

13: "Enquires Communicated." Alexandria Gazette, December 12, 1870.

14: Robinson, John. "General Assembly Passes Ficklin Bill." *The Richmond Times-Dispatch*, January 11, 1871.

Chapter 3: Firing the Locomotives

1: Information on Thomas Nevitt from the research files of the Franconia Museum, Inc., 6121 Franconia Road, Alexandria. Filed under Lorton, original source unknown.

2: Lee, Nathaniel. "Nevitt Street Sign" 2016. JPEG file. Photograph taken by the author.

3: Wreb, Jon E. "The Mysterious Southern Porcelain Company." Crown Jewels of the Wire. August 1997. http://www.cjow.com/archive/article.php?month=88a=08The%20Mysterious%20Southern%20Porcelain%20Company.htm&year=1997. Accessed January 16, 2016.

4: Lee, Nathaniel. "Telegraph Road Station 1872 map." 2015. PNG file. Drawn using the open data service from Fairfax County's Geographic Information System and Mapping Service Branch, Fairfax, Virginia. Accessed September 23, 2015. http://www.fairfaxcounty.gov/maps.

5: Lee, Nathaniel. "Telegraph Road Station 1872 map." 2015. PNG file. Drawn using the open data service from Fairfax County's Geographic Information System and Mapping Service Branch, Fairfax, Virginia. Accessed September 23, 2015. http://www.fairfaxcounty.gov/maps.

6: Lee, Nathaniel. "Old Telegraph Line roadside marker." 2006. JPEG file. Photograph taken by the author.

7: Costa, Tom. "George Mason and Pohick Church." George Mason's Gunston Hall. January 23, 2014. http://gunstonhallblog.blogspot.com/2014/01/george-mason-and-pohick-church.html. Accessed January 16, 2016.

8: Roberts, Jay. "Geo Quiz: Major Tributary Streams of the Potomac." Jaybird's Jottings. September 17, 2014. http://jay.typepad.com/william_jay/2014/09/geo-quiz-major-tributary-streams-of-the-potomac.html. Accessed January 16, 2016.

9: Lee, Nathaniel. "Pohick Stop 1872 map." 2015. PNG file. Drawn using the open data service from Fairfax County's Geographic Information System and Mapping Service Branch, Fairfax, Virginia. Accessed September 28, 2015. http://www.fairfaxcounty.gov/maps.

10: Lee, Nathaniel. "Accotink Station 1872 map." 2015. PNG file. Drawn using the open data service from Fairfax County's Geographic Information System and Mapping Service Branch, Fairfax, Virginia. Accessed September 28, 2015. http://www.fairfaxcounty.gov/maps.

11: "Local Affairs." Alexandria Gazette, April 1, 1872.

12: Lee, Nathaniel. "Long Branch Station 1872 map." 2015. PNG file. Drawn using the open data service from Fairfax County's Geographic Information System and Mapping Service Branch, Fairfax, Virginia. Accessed September 21, 2015. http://www.fairfaxcounty.gov/maps.

13: Lee, Nathaniel. "Newington roadside marker." 2006. JPEG file. Photograph taken by the author.

14: Harrison, Fairfax. "Landmarks of Old Prince William: A Study of Origins in Northern Virginia." Berryville, Virginia: Chesapeake Book Company, 1964.

15: Lee, Nathaniel. "Ravenworth Stop 1872 map." 2015. PNG file. Drawn using the open data service from Fairfax County's Geographic Information System and Mapping Service Branch, Fairfax, Virginia. Accessed September 20, 2015. http://www.fairfaxcounty.gov/maps.

16: "Anna Maria Fitzhugh." Anna Maria Fitzhugh Chapter of the Virginia Daughters of the American Revolution. Accessed October 13, 2015. http://annamariafitzhugh.vadar.org/anna-maria-fitzhugh.html. Picture used with permission of Terri Spencer.

17: Nagel, Paul C. "The Lees of Virginia: Seven Generations of an American Family." Oxford, England: Oxford University Press. 1992. Information of Anna Fitzhugh.

18: Photograph of the Ravensworth mansion comes from archive files of the Franconia Museum, 6121 Franconia Road, Alexandria, Virginia. Original photographer unknown.

19: Lee, Nathaniel. "Ravensworth roadside marker." 2005. JPEG file. Photograph taken by the author.

20: Freeman, Douglas S. "George Washington: A Biography." 6 volumes. New York, New York: Charles Scribner's Sons, 1951.

21: Lee, Nathaniel. "Windsor Stop 1872 map." 2015. PNG file. Drawn using the open data service from Fairfax County's Geographic Information System and Mapping Service Branch, Fairfax, Virginia. Accessed September 20, 2015. http://www.fairfaxcounty.gov/maps.

22: McGroarty, William Buckner. "Elizabeth Washington of Hayfield." Richmond, Virginia: Virginia Magazine of History and Biography. 1925. Information on the Hayfield property.

23: United States Congress. "The War of the Rebellion: A Compilation of the Official records of the Union and Confederate Armies. 128 volumes. Second series. Washington, District of Columbia: Government Printing Office, 1880-1910.

24: Lee, Nathaniel. "Franconia Station 1872 map." 2015. PNG file. Drawn using the open data service from Fairfax County's Geographic Information System and Mapping Service Branch, Fairfax, Virginia. Accessed September 20, 2015. http://www.fairfaxcounty.gov/maps.

25: Lee, Nathaniel. "Franconia roadside marker." 2013. JPEG file. Photograph taken by the author.

26: Lee, Nathaniel. "Bush Hill Stop 1872 map." 2015. PNG file. Drawn using the open data service from Fairfax County's Geographic Information System and Mapping Service Branch, Fairfax, Virginia. Accessed September 28, 2015. http://www.fairfaxcounty.gov/maps.

27: Hakenson, Don. "This Forgotten Land: A tour of Civil War sites and other historical landmarks south of Alexandria, Virginia." 1st ed. Alexandria, Virginia. 2002. Photograph of Bush Hill manor house used with permission from the author.

28: "The Glory and the Grandeur." Army Material Command News (Alexandria), April 1990. Information on the Bush Hill estate.

29: Lee, Nathaniel. "Virginia Midland crossing map." 2016. PNG file. Drawn using the open data service from Fairfax County's Geographic Information System and Mapping Service Branch, Fairfax, Virginia. Accessed January 17, 2016. http://www.fairfaxcounty.gov/maps.

30: Lee, Nathaniel. "Seminary Stop 1872 map." 2015. PNG file. Drawn using the open data service from Fairfax County's Geographic Information System and Mapping Service Branch, Fairfax, Virginia. Accessed September 28, 2015. http://www.fairfaxcounty.gov/maps.

31: Detroit Publishing Company. "Theological Seminary [i.e. Protestant Episcopal Theological Seminary], Alexandria, Va." The Library of Congress. 1900. Dry plate negative. Accessed November 22, 2015. http://www.loc.gov/resource/det.4a13118.

32: Dallzell, George W. "Benefit of Clergy in America and Related Matters." Winston-Salem, North Carolina: John F. Blair Publishing, 1955. Information on the Episcopal Seminary.

33: Lee, Nathaniel. "Fayette Street Railroad marker." 2015. JPEG file. Photograph taken by the author.

34: Lee, Nathaniel. "Bastille AnW rails." 2015. JPEG file. Photograph taken by the author.

35: "P. R. R. Standard Passenger Shelter for Branch Roads." Document is in the public domain and comes courtesy of Rob Schoenburg and the Pennsylvania Railroad Technical and Historical Society, Post Office Box 54, Bryn Mawr, Pennsylvania 19010.

36: Photograph of R. F. & P. Railroad engine number 307 at Franconia Station taken by Bruce Fales and comes courtesy of the Richmond, Fredericksburg and Potomac Historical Society, Inc., Post Office Box 9097, Fredericksburg, Virginia 22403-9097.

37: "Alexandria and Fredericksburg Railway." The Evening Star (Washington), May 22, 1872. Evening edition.

38: Pennsylvania Railroad Company. Instructions for making Reports to the Car Record Office, abbreviations to be used when reporting cars; numbers and names of stations and sidings; Alphabetical list of stations and sidings, with location and names of agents; list of

Supervisors, Train-Masters and Yard Masters, with location and extent of jurisdiction; also, alphabetical list of scales, with names of weighmasters, and list of numbers and classification of cars. Philadelphia. 1884.

39: Desty, Robert. The Supreme Court Reporter, Volume 15, National reporter System, United States series. Minneapolis, Minnesota: West Publishing Company. 1895. Information on court cases brought against the Pennsylvania Railroad.

40: Netherton, Nan, Donald Sweig, Janice Artemel, Patricia Hickin and Patrick Reed. "Fairfax County, Virginia: A History." Fairfax, Virginia: Fairfax County Board of Supervisors. 1978. Information on railroad development in Fairfax County.

41: Kamm, Samuel Richey. "The Civil War Career of Thomas A. Scott." Philadelphia, Pennsylvania: University of Pennsylvania Press. 1940.

42: Carnegie, Andrew. "Autobiography of Andrew Carnegie." Edited by John Charles Van Dyke. London: Constable and Company, Limited. 1920. Image of Thomas Alexander Scott is in the public domain and comes courtesy of Michael Hart and Project Gutenburg.

43: Cohen, Robert. "History of the Long Bridge." Washington, District of Columbia: Timetable Press. 2003.

44: "A Railroad Runs Through It." Historical Marker Database. February 9, 2008. Accessed December 19, 2015. http://www.hmdb.org/marker.asp?marker=5252.

45: French, Herbert A. "Long Bridge across the Potomac River, 1865." Glass negative. Washington, District of Columbia: National Photo Company. From the Library of Congress. http://hdl.loc.gov/loc.pnp/npcc.30375. Photograph is in the public domain and comes from the Library of Congress Prints and Photographs Division.

46: Photograph of the Alexandria and Fredericksburg train on Franconia Grade comes courtesy of James Musgrove and the Richmond, Fredericksburg and Potomac Historical Society, Inc., Post Office Box 9097, Fredericksburg, Virginia 22403-9097.

47: Gardner, Alexander. Photographer. "Acquia (i.e. Aquia) Creek Landing, Va." Albumen print. Washington, District of Columbia: Center for Civil War Photography. From the Library of Congress. http://hdl.loc.gov/loc.pnp/ppmsca.33253. Photograph is in the public domain and comes from the Library of Congress Prints and Photographs Division.

48: "The Potomac Boats on the Richmond Route." Evening Star (Washington), May 12, 1881. Evening edition.

Chapter 4: Washington Southern

1: "G.B. Roberts." Engraving. Jersey City, New Jersey: Railroad Topics Company. 1890. From Library of Congress. http://www.loc.gov/item/91482950. Engraving of George Brooke Roberts is in the public domain and comes courtesy of the Library of Congress, Prints and Photographs Division.

2: The American and English Railroad Cases: A Collection of All Cases, Affecting Railroads of Every Kind, Decided by the Courts of Appellate Jurisdiction in the United States, England, and Canada [1894-1913]. E. Thomson Company, 1916. Information on the Alexandria and Washington Railway court cases.

3: Use of the photograph of the Lorton station house comes with the permission of Bob Koch of the Lorton Historical Society.

4: Mitchell, Beth. "Fairfax County Road Orders 1749-1800." Charlottesville, Virginia: University of Virginia Press. 2003. In-depth analysis of the colonial roadways.

5: Lee, Nathaniel. "Accotink 1890 map." 2015. PNG file. Drawn using the open data service from Fairfax County's Geographic Information System and Mapping Service Branch, Fairfax, Virginia. Accessed September 21, 2015. http://www.fairfaxcounty.gov/maps.

6: Lee, Nathaniel. "Lorton Station roadside marker." 2008. JPEG file. Photograph taken by the author.

7: Lee, Nathaniel. "Pohick Stop 1890 map." 2015. PNG file. Drawn using the open data service from Fairfax County's Geographic Information System and Mapping Service Branch, Fairfax, Virginia. Accessed September 21, 2015. http://www.fairfaxcounty.gov/maps.

8: Lee, Nathaniel. "Pohick Stop No 1 1890 map." 2015. PNG file. Drawn using the open data service from Fairfax County's Geographic Information System and Mapping Service Branch, Fairfax, Virginia. Accessed September 21, 2015. http://www.fairfaxcounty.gov/maps.

9: Lee, Nathaniel. "Pohick Stop No 2 1890 map." 2015. PNG file. Drawn using the open data service from Fairfax County's Geographic Information System and Mapping Service Branch, Fairfax, Virginia. Accessed September 28, 2015. http://www.fairfaxcounty.gov/maps.

10: Lee, Nathaniel. "Gravel Stop 1890 map." 2015. PNG file. Drawn using the open data service from Fairfax County's Geographic Information System and Mapping Service Branch, Fairfax, Virginia. Accessed September 20, 2015. http://www.fairfaxcounty.gov/maps.

11: Lee, Nathaniel. "Burgundy 1890 map." 2015. PNG file. Drawn using the open data service from Fairfax County's Geographic Information System and Mapping Service Branch, Fairfax, Virginia. Accessed September 26, 2015. http://www.fairfaxcounty.gov/maps.

12: Photograph of the Burgundy mansion comes from archive files of the Franconia Museum, 6121 Franconia Road, Alexandria, Virginia. Original photographer unknown.

13: Pennsylvania Railroad Company. List of Stations and Sidings and Instructions for Making Reports to the Car Record Office. Philadelphia. 1900.

14: "Death of Frank Thomson: President of the Pennsylvania Railroad Expires Suddenly." The New York Times. June 6, 1899. Accessed January 18, 2016. http://article.archive.nytimes.com/1899/06/06/118937888.pdf.

15: Jacobs, Timothy. "History of the Pennsylvania Railroad." Greenville, South Carolina: Crescent Publishing Group. 1988. Information on Alexander Cassett.

16: King, Moses. King's views of the New York stock exchange. Boston, Massachusetts: M. King. 1898. Electronic reproduction. New York, New York: Columbia University Libraries, 2008. Engraving of Frank Thomas is in the public domain and comes courtesy of Columbia University Libraries Digital Collections.

17: The World's Work, Volume II, May 1901 – October 1901: A History of Our Time. Vol. 2. New York, New York: Doubleday, Page and Company. 1901. Electronic reproduction. Toronto, Canada: University of Toronto Press, 2010. Image of Alexander Cassatt is in the public domain and comes courtesy of the University of Toronto's Robarts Library.

18: Prince, Richard E. "The Richmond-Washington Line and related railroads: Florida Fast Line, capital cities route. Prince. 1973. Information on the formation of the Richmond-Washington Line.

19: Mordecai, John B. "A Brief History of the Richmond, Fredericksburg and Potomac Railroad." Richmond, Virginia: Old Dominion Publishing, 1941. Information on the beginning of the Richmond-Washington Company.

20: Richmond-Washington Company. Richmond, Fredericksburg and Potomac Railroad and Washington Southern Railway between Richmond and Washington and Intermediate Points. Richmond, Virginia: Richmond-Washington Company. 1912. Used with permission from Mr. Lucas Clawson and The Hagley Museum and Library Manuscripts and Archives Department, 298 Buck Road East, Greenville, Delaware 19807.

21: Griffin, William E. Jr., "One Hundred Fifty Years of History: Along the Richmond, Fredericksburg and Potomac Railroad." Richmond, Fredericksburg and Potomac Railroad Company: Richmond, Virginia. 1984.

22: Bryant, Tammy. "Documentary Study of the 1300 Block of Duke Street, Alexandria, Virginia." Gainesville, Virginia: Thunderbird Archaeology. 2007.

23: Sheild, William. "Potomac Yard, VA: The Gateway Between the North and the South, Book 2." Fredericksburg, Virginia: The Richmond, Fredericksburg and Potomac Railroad Historical Society, Inc. 2015. Information on the operation of Potomac Yard.

Chapter 5: Railroad Realignment

1: "Terrific Explosion Startles Residents of Franconia." The Evening Star (Washington), May 21, 1904. Evening edition.

2: Hakenson, Don. "This Forgotten Land: A tour of Civil War sites and other historical landmarks south of Alexandria, Virginia." 1st ed. Alexandria, Virginia. 2002. Information on the Fort Lyon accident.

3: "City and District." The Evening Star (Washington), September 26, 1905. Evening edition.

4: District of Columbia. Court of Appeals. "Reports of Cases Adjudged in the Court of Appeals of the District of Columbia from June 6, 1892-Dec. 18, 1933, Volume 30." Washington, District of Columbia: West Publishing Company. 1908. 560. Information on the Glaria Supreme Court case.

5: Lee, Nathaniel. "Colchester 1903 map." 2015. PNG file. Drawn using the open data service from Fairfax County's Geographic Information System and Mapping Service Branch, Fairfax, Virginia. Accessed October 22, 2015. http://www.fairfaxcounty.gov/maps.

6: Davis, John. "Colchester Inn, 10712 Old Colchester Road, Lorton, Fairfax County, VA." The Library of Congress. 1933. 7 photographs. Accessed November 24, 2015. http://lccn.loc.gov/item/va0432. Artwork is in the public domain and comes from the Library of Congress Prints and Photographs Division, Washington, D.C.

7: Lee, Nathaniel. "Pohick Stop 1903 map." 2015. PNG file. Drawn using the open data service from Fairfax County's Geographic Information System and Mapping Service Branch, Fairfax, Virginia. Accessed September 21, 2015. http://www.fairfaxcounty.gov/maps.

8: Lee, Nathaniel. "Accotink Station 1903 map." 2015. PNG file. Drawn using the open data service from Fairfax County's Geographic Information System and Mapping Service Branch, Fairfax, Virginia. Accessed September 28, 2015. http://www.fairfaxcounty.gov/maps.

9: Sell, Carl and Jim Cox. "The Franconia Museum Presents Franconia Remembers The Franconia Volunteer Fire Department." Alexandria, Virginia: Franconia Museum, Inc. 2012. Information regarding fire department participation in the fatal crash of 1972.

10: Lee, Nathaniel. "Franconia Station 1903 map." 2015. PNG file. Drawn using the open data service from Fairfax County's Geographic Information System and Mapping Service Branch, Fairfax, Virginia. Accessed September 20, 2015. http://www.fairfaxcounty.gov/maps.

11: Photograph of the Franconia train station used with the permission of Franconia Museum, Inc., 6121 Franconia Road, Alexandria, Virginia 22310.

12: Lee, Nathaniel. "Lunt Stop 1905 map." 2015. PNG file. Drawn using the open data service from Fairfax County's Geographic Information System and Mapping Service Branch, Fairfax, Virginia. Accessed September 20, 2015. http://www.fairfaxcounty.gov/maps.

13: Lee, Nathaniel. "Lunt Pharmacy." 2009. JPEG file. Photograph taken by the author.

14: Lee, Nathaniel. "Bush Hill Stop 1905 map." 2015. PNG file. Drawn using the open data service from Fairfax County's Geographic Information System and Mapping Service Branch, Fairfax, Virginia. Accessed September 20, 2015. http://www.fairfaxcounty.gov/maps.

15: Lee, Nathaniel. "Seminary Stop 1905 map." 2015. PNG file. Drawn using the open data service from Fairfax County's Geographic Information System and Mapping Service Branch, Fairfax, Virginia. Accessed September 20, 2015. http://www.fairfaxcounty.gov/maps.

16: Hakenson, Don. "This Forgotten Land: A tour of Civil War sites and other historical landmarks south of Alexandria, Virginia." 1st ed. Alexandria, Virginia. 2002. Photograph of Bush Hill bridge used with permission from the author.

17: Musgrove, Jim. "Riding the RF&P South of Alexandria Along the Franconia Grade." *The Richmond, Fredericksburg and Potomac Historical Society, Inc.* 7, no. 1 (Winter 2011): 3-8.

18: "Local News." Alexandria Gazette, April 15, 1872.

19: Griffin, William E. Jr. "One Hundred Fifty Years of History: Along the Richmond, Fredericksburg and Potomac Railroad." Richmond: Richmond, Fredericksburg and Potomac Railroad Co., 1984.

20: Pennypacker, Samuel Whitaker. "Annals of Phoenixville And Its Vicinity." Bavis and Pennypacker: Philadelphia, Pennsylvania. 1872. Information regarding the Phoenix Iron Company and Steel Company.

21: Kirkpatrick, Bob. "Occoquan Park view of Bridge." 2012. JPEG file. Photograph used with the permission of the Franconia Museum, Inc.

22: "Mrs. Mary Gorham Killed By Passenger Train." The Evening Star (Washington), October 14, 1904. Evening edition.

23: Photograph of R. F. & P. Railroad engine number 502 at Franconia Road Overpass comes courtesy of Jim Musgrove and the Richmond, Fredericksburg and Potomac Historical Society, Inc., Post Office Box 9097, Fredericksburg, Virginia 22403-9097.

24: "Sacrifices Her Life For Her Son." Richmond Times-Dispatch, October 15, 1904.

Chapter 6: "I Am Not in Denial!"

1: "Another Tragedy at a Fatal Grade Crossing." The Evening Star (Washington), July 10, 1899, evening edition. Information on John Nevitt.

2: "Girl Killed by Train." The Richmond Times-Dispatch, November 14, 1916. Information on Osie Rogers.

3: "Rail Worker Is Killed By R., F. & P. Train." The Richmond Times-Dispatch, May 5, 1923. Information on Wallace Hopkins.

4: "Alexandria Man Killed By Train." The Evening Star (Washington), October 3, 1979, evening edition. Information on John Boggs.

5: "A Frightful Collision." The Evening Star (Washington), August 2, 1899, evening edition. Information on Jeremiah Desmond.

6: French, Herbert A. "Train wreck at Cameron Run." Photograph. Washington, District of Columbia: National Photo Company. 1926. From the Library of Congress. Accessed November 15, 2015. http://hdl.loc.gov/loc.pnp/npcc.16074. Photograph is in the public domain and comes from the Library of Congress Prints and Photographs Division.

7: "Alexandria Affairs." The Evening Star (Washington), April 13, 1901. Evening edition. Information on the express car robbery.

8: Reynolds, Keith. "Safe from the Wilcox train robbery." Photograph. Laramie, Wyoming: Univ. of Wyoming. 1899. Accessed November 24, 2015. http://digital.uwyo.edu/thumbs.cfm?collection=ah_order&img=ah002995.jpg. Photograph is in the public domain and comes from the American Heritage Center, Laramie, Wyoming.

9: "Walter D. Hines, bust portrait." Photograph. Washington, District of Columbia: Harris and Ewing Company. 1919. Accessed November 26, 2015. http://hdl.loc.gov/loc.pnp/cph.3a42961. Photograph is in the public domain and comes from the Library of Congress Prints and Photographs Division.

10: U.S. Senate Hearings: Government Control and Operation of Railroads. 1918. 65th Congress, 2nd session, CXVII. Committee on Interstate Commerce. Washington, D.C. Information on the government's view of proximate cause and liability.

11: Krauss, Michael I., Rape on the Washington Southern: The Tragic Case of Hines v. Garrett (December 4, 2009). George Mason Law & Economics Research Paper No. 09-63. Available at SSRN: http://ssrn.com/abstract=1518630.

12: Hines v. Garrett. Supreme Court of Appeals of Virginia. Brief in behalf of defendant-in-error. 312 Records and Briefs, Supreme Court of Appeals at Richmond. Richmond, Virginia.

13: "28 Freight Cars Are Derailed Near Lorton, Trains Delayed." The Evening Star (Washington), February 6, 1955. Information on the fruit spill accident.

14: "25 Persons Are Injured In Train Crash." The Richmond Times-Dispatch, July 24, 1942. Information on the Fort Belvoir train wreck.

16: "Another Train Victim Is Identified." The Richmond Times-Dispatch, January 29, 1970. Information on crash causes.

17: Bredemeier, Kenneth and Gordon Pettey. "Track Slippage Blamed." The Washington Post, January 28, 1970, sec. C. Photograph by Jim McNamara.

18: McDowell Jr., Charles. "N.Y.-Bound Train Derails, Three Killed, 57 Injured." Morning Star, January 28, 1970, sec. A. Accessed September 23, 2015. http://www.geneologybank.com/dpc/newspapers/image/v2%3A12B9.

19: McDowell Jr., Charles. "RF&P Train Wreck Inquiry Yields Safety Device Theory." The Richmond Times-Dispatch, March 26, 1970. Information on train wreck causes.

20: Photograph of baggage handler from the archive files of the Franconia Museum, 6121 Franconia Road, Alexandria, Virginia 22310. Original photographer unknown.

21: Bredemeier, Kenneth and Gordon Pettey. "Track Slippage Blamed." The Washington Post, January 28, 1970, sec. C. Photograph by Robert Milnes.

22: Waugh, William J., "Derailment in Virginia Kills 3." The Mobile Register. January 28, 1970. Information on train derailment and quote from Shumate.

Chapter 7: The Way Things Work

1: Kapoor, Ajay and Mark Robinson, ed. "Fatigue in Railway Infrastructure." Sawston, Cambridge: Woodhead Publishing. 2009. Information on forces of nature at play.

2: Pike, Jim. "Track." Stroud, Gloucestershire, England: Sutton Publishing Limited. 2001. Information on the use of ballast.

3: "Rails and Ballast." Digital image. Wikimedia Commons. March 6, 2005. Accessed December 30, 2015. https://commons.m.wikimedia.org/wiki/File:Rails.and.ballast.bb.jpg#mw-jump-to-license. Photographer has released image to public domain.

4: Olofsson, Ron. "Wheel-Rail Interface Handbook." Sawston, Cambridge: Woodhead Publishing. 2009. Information on how trains stay on the tracks.

5: Brown, Oliver. "Railway turnout with electric throw." Digital image. Wikimedia Commons. April 30, 2006. Accessed January 23, 2016. https://commons.m.wikimedia.org/wiki/File:Railway_turnout_with_electric_throw.jpg. Photographer has released photograph to public domain.

6: Puta, Roger and Marty Bernard. "RF&P 1007 with Train 33, The Silver Comet, passing AF tower, Alexandria, VA on March 23, 1969." Digital image. Flickr. March 23, 1969. Accessed January 23, 2016. https://www.flickr.com/photos/129679309@N05/24731746229. Photographer has released the photograph to the public domain.

7: Union Switch and Signal Company. "e17749." Digital image. Railway Mail Service Library. 1921. Accessed December 12, 2015. http://www.railwaymailservicelibrary.org/aftower/aftower.htm. Photograph from Jim Musgrove and the Richmond, Fredericksburg and Potomac Historical Society, Inc., Post Office Box 9097, Fredericksburg, Virginia 22403-9097.

8: Photograph of the interlock tower at Pohick Creek comes from archive files of the Franconia Museum, 6121 Franconia Road, Alexandria, Virginia. Original photographer unknown.

Chapter 8: The Line Earns Its Spurs

1: Bernikow, Louisa. "Night of Terror Leads to Women's Vote in 1917." Womens ENews. October 30, 2004. http://womensenews.org/2004/10/night-terror-leads-womens-vote-1917/#.Us2mpUko6M8.

3: Thomas, Charles B. "The Lorton and Occoquan Railroad." *The Richmond, Fredericksburg and Potomac Historical Society, Inc.* 5, no. 1 (Winter 2009): 7-10.

4: Map of the Lorton and Occoquan Railway line comes from the archive files of the Franconia Museum, Inc., 6121 Franconia Road, Alexandria, VA 22310.

5: Milner, John. "District of Columbia Workhouse and Reformatory National Register Nomination." Charlottesville, Virginia: John Milner Associates, Incorporated. 2005.

6: Lee, Nathaniel. "Prison Boxcar." 2011. JPEG file. Photograph taken by the author.

7: Lee, Nathaniel. "Barrel Bridge from the trail." 2011. JPEG file. Photograph taken by the author.

8: Muir, Dorothy T. "Potomac Interlude: The Story of Woodlawn Mansion and the Mount Vernon neighborhood 1846-1943." Washington, District of Columbia: Mount Vernon Print Shop. 1943.

9: Carlson, George L. "The U.S. Engineers Need You." Lithograph. Heywood, Strasser and Voigt Lithograph Company: New York, New York. 1917. Accessed November 16, 2015. http://www.loc.gov/item/2002708930/. This lithograph is in the public domain and comes from the Library of Congress Prints and Photographs Division, Washington, DC.

10: Sprouse, Edith Moore "Mount Air." Fairfax, Virginia: Fairfax County Office of Comprehensive Planning. 1976. Information on the involvement of Mount Air property in the creation of Camp Humphreys.

11: "The Official History of the Three Hundred and Fourth Engineer Regiment, Seventy-ninth Division, U.S.A.: During the World War." Lancaster, Pennsylvania: Press of Steinman and Foltz. 1919. Photograph is in the public domain as the copyright has expired.

12: Image of engine on Camp Humphrey's light railway from the research archives of the Franconia Museum, 6121 Franconia Road, Alexandria, VA 22310. Official government publication, original photographer unknown.

13: Image of supply depot for Camp Humphrey's light railway comes from the research archives of the Franconia Museum, 6121 Franconia Road, Alexandria, VA 22310. Official government publication, original photographer unknown.

Chapter 9: The Modern Era

1: Mordecai, John B. "Richmond, Fredericksburg and Potomac Railroad in the Second World War." No Publisher. 1948. Information on the war years.

2: Wilson, Debbie, ed. "Olivet Episcopal Chapel Bell Rung by Hand Each Sunday." Historic Franconia Legacies, Fall 2015, 5. Photograph of chapel used with permission from the Franconia Museum, Inc., 6121 Franconia Road, Franconia, Virginia 22310.

3: Carper, Robert S. "American Railroads in Transition: The Passing of the Steam Locomotives." Saint Marie, England: Barnes Publishing Limited. 1968.

4: "Why Are Richmond-Washington Trains Late? RF&P Has Problems." The Richmond Times-Dispatch, May 1, 1949. Information on the RF&P switchover to diesel and reduction in service following the Second World War.

5: Photograph of the Parr Warehouses from the research archives of the Franconia Museum, Inc., 6121 Franconia Road, Franconia, Virginia 22310. Photograph is unmarked, believed to be part of the county aerial survey.

6: Bell, A.H. Location and Design Engineer. "The Henry G. Shirley Memorial Highway." Virginia Department of Highways, published in Virginia Road Builder, January 1946. Photograph is in the public domain and used with permission from the Virginia Department of Transportation.

7: Lee, Nathaniel. "Amtrak train and temple." 2009. JPEG file. Photograph taken by the author.

8: "Rail service has busy past, study may spur new service." The Fairfax Sentinel, June 17, 1971. Information on approval of New Franconia development and approval.

9: Ely, Wally. "Auto-Train (Images of Rail)." Raleigh, North Carolina: Arcadia Publishing Company. 2009. Information on the Auto Train company over the years.

10: Photograph of the Lorton Auto-Train terminal from the research archives of the Franconia Museum, Inc., 6121 Franconia Road, Franconia, Virginia 22310 and used with permission. Original photographer remains unknown.

11: Lukasiewicz, Julius. "The Railway Game." Ottawa, Ontario: Carleton University Press. 1976. Information on the operation of the Auto Train.

12: "New Towns." The Evening Star (Washington), May 18, 1973. Information on approval of New Franconia development and approval.

13: "Future for a Gravel Pit." The Richmond Times-Dispatch, May 1, 1949. Information on the monorail on the New Franconia site.

14: "Franconia Developer Giving Up?" The Evening Star (Washington), January 26, 1973. Article features a map of the proposed development site.

15: "Cars Not Needed in Fairfax Town." The Richmond Times-Dispatch, March 19, 1972. Article speaks about the Fairfax County Board of Supervisors.

16: Bertsch, Amy and Lance Mallamo. "Out of the Attic." Alexandria Times, April 16, 2009. Photograph used with permission from the Office of Historic Alexandria, 220 North Washington Street, Alexandria, Virginia 22314.

17: Frye, John. "Birds on a Wire." *The Richmond, Fredericksburg and Potomac Historical Society, Inc.* 8, no. 4 (Fall 2012): 13.

18: "240-Foot Tower Gets County Hearing On Nov. 8." The Alexandria Gazette, November 7, 1978. Information on the radio communications tower.

19: Lee, Nathaniel. "Joe Alexander exclusive talk." 2015. JPEG file. Photograph taken by the author.

20: "Tower Advances." The Alexandria Gazette, November 10, 1978. Information about the microwave tower installed near Valley View.

21: "CSX Could Get RF&P Rail Link." The Washington Post, March 12, 1984. Information on the CSX merger.

22: Rogers, J. "Generals of the Confederate Army, No. 2: J.E.B. Stuart, Earl Van Dorn, J.C. Breckinridge, N.B. Forrest, W.J. Hardee." Engraving. New York, New York: Virtue and Yorston Company. 1866. Accessed November 30, 2015. http://lccn.loc.gov/2003673102. Photograph of Earl Van Dorn is in the public domain and comes from the Library of Congress Prints and Photographs Division, Washington, District of Columbia.

23: Johnson, Matt and David Alpert. "The Metro Plan Has Changed a Lot since 1968." Greater Greater Washington. July 14, 2014. Accessed January 4, 2016. Information on early stations planned at Backlick and Franconia.

24: Taube, Richard K. "Chronology of the Virginia Railway Express." Alexandria, Virginia: Virginia Railway Express. 2008.

25: Lee, Nathaniel. "VRE train at Franconia." 2015. JPEG file. Photograph taken by the author.

26: Tucker, Matthew. "Washington, DC to Richmond Third Track Feasibility Study." Richmond, Virginia: Department of Rail and Public Transportation. 2006.

27: Beadles, Richard L. "Railroad Policy In Virginia: How We Got Where We Are and Where We Might Go From Here." *The Virginia News Letter*, June 2013.

28: Testerman, Michael. "Review of Virginia's Rail Enhancement Fund." Virginia Rail Policy Institute. 2014. Accessed January 4, 2016. http://varpi.org/node/38.

29: Booker, Cory. "Democratic Platform Committee." Speech, Democratic National Convention, Charlotte, North Carolina, September 4, 2012.

Chapter Twelve

GENERAL INDEX

ℰℭ

*"One may take a journey of any
distance at any time, if he simply
chooses to ride a train of thought."*
– LaTonya Tarrell

ℰℭ

G

ABOUT THE AUTHOR

NATHANIEL CAREY LEE is not old enough to have seen all the important Franconia landmarks of days gone by, but he sure knows where they were located. Serving as a member of the Franconia Museum's Board of Directors and museum docent, Nathaniel is a great resource when memories get fuzzy. In fact, he has documented their location on a hand-drawn map that blends the old and the new in the Franconia community. It has already become an important tool when visitors to the Franconia Museum. Nathaniel's family has lived here in the Franconia community for three generations, watching the area transform. He grew up next to Franconia Elementary School, which he attended, along with Mark Twain Middle School and Robert E. Lee High School. Nathaniel now lives next to the railroad in this book, and loves to hear the sound of a train rumbling past in the night.

FRANCONIA MUSEUM

The Franconia Museum, Inc. is a 501(c)(3) tax-exempt volunteer organization incorporated under the laws of the Commonwealth of Virginia. The Museum itself is located inside the Franconia Governmental Center at 6121 Franconia Road, Franconia, Virginia 22310. A Board of Directors, all of whom are volunteers, runs the Museum. Operating funds are raised through memberships, tours and sales of books.

Formed in 2002, The Franconia Museum is a local history museum dedicated to preserving the past, present and future of the Franconia area in its pictures, artifacts and stories. It is difficult to imagine looking across eight lanes of traffic on Franconia Road, that it was once a rural "rolling road" for Virginia tobacco on its way to the port city of Alexandria, the birthplace of the only state governor from Northern Virginia, witness to Civil War raids and home to a thriving African-American community called Carrolltown. Become a friend today by visiting us online at www.FranconiaMuseum.org.

Franconia Museum, Inc.

6121 Franconia Road
Alexandria, Virginia 22310

Hours of Operation:
10:00 a.m. to 2:00 p.m.
Mon., Tues., Wed. and Sat.
Open other times by appointment.